To Christy,

In celebration of
parents, teachers &
students!

T. Andrews
&
Becky Saarela

Sincerely, The Teacher: The Top 10 Things Teachers Want Parents to Know

Edited by Andrea Shupert
Cover and website design by Jared Erickson

Student/parent/teachers' names and details of their stories have been
changed, fictionalized, and intermingled to protect their identities.

ISBN-978-0-557-30210-9

www.sincerelytheteacher.com

Sincerely, The Teacher

The Top 10 Things Teachers Want Parents to Know

By: Tiffany Andrews & Becky Saarela

Table of Contents

PAGE 6 | Introduction

PAGE 13 | #1 Graduation starts in kindergarten
Position your child for a successful future.

PAGE 24 | #2 You choose the cycle
Be a positive influence on your child's school journey.

PAGE 36 | #3 We are all on the same team
Parents and teachers must come together to be a powerhouse support for the students.

PAGE 48 | #4 Lend a helping hand
A parent's help means that teachers can spend more time on creating interactive lessons for the students.

PAGE 60 | #5 Manners do matter
Manners are a skill learned early but practiced throughout life.

PAGE 70 | #6 A compliment goes a long way
Select the words you say to your child; don't just say them.

PAGE 79 | #7 Stand strong as a parent
Children need clear, consistent boundaries in life to feel secure.

PAGE 89 | #8 Practice T-R-U-S-T

Trust the professional experience and advice of teachers.

PAGE 103 | #9 Know your child's learning style

The area where your child thrives in school is the area where you can build success.

PAGE 115 | #10 Parents are the common denominator

What to do each step of the way in your child's school journey.

PAGE 132 | Conclusion

PAGE 134 | Cheat Sheet of Educational Terms

Introduction

"A teacher is… like my mom."
~Kindergarten student

I asked my kindergarten students:
"How much time do we spend in school each day?"
Here were some of their responses:
"1 minute!"
"6 days!"
"40 hours!"
"A *long* time."

As accurate as the students' responses were, the truth is a student spends approximately 8 hours a day in school. That averages to about 1440 hours per year, or 86,400 minutes spent away from home in a school setting. By the time a student reaches his senior year of high school it could be up to 17,280 hours of time spent in a school environment. This total does not even include time spent on homework or extracurricular activities, so one can imagine what those numbers may add up to! After my first year of teaching, I quickly realized how much time a teacher spends with her students. It didn't take much calculating to figure out that I spent more time with my students than I do with my husband or my family.

As a parent you might already be aware that your child spends a lot of time in school, but to see the numbers written in black and white makes it even more profound. However you may not know that even though your child spends considerable amounts of time with his teacher it does not change one very important fact: *you are the most important factor in your child's education*. Each school year your child gets a new teacher but who are the common denominators? *The parents*. Teachers are only in your childrens' lives for a season of their lives. No matter how much a teacher cares for a student the ultimate educator is you, the parent.

Teachers view themselves as the professionals who are willing and available to provide parents with guidance to help their children succeed in the classroom. Just as doctors are important to families for their health, teachers are important for families and the wellness of the children's education. For example, if you have a sick child, the first person you turn to is a doctor. In turn, the doctor gives you tips and advice that you can do at home in order to get your child well. For many years, doctors have been writing books about topics like at-home healthcare, tips to staying fit, ways to avoid diseases, and how to raise a healthy child. Many concerned parents have found their health answers merely by picking up one of these helpful books. I was shocked to discover when I went to into a bookstore and looked up "education"; about 95% or more of the books are written for teachers. Of course, teachers need those books to better themselves professionally, but where is a book to help parents? Parents also need strategies, ideas, and tools available to them. Our hearts' desire is that this book will provide those strategies, ideas, and tools.

"This is a guide for parents to use in the midst of their children's journey through school."

The idea for *Sincerely, The Teacher* came one afternoon during my commute home from work. At the time I had a challenging student, and like many commutes home, I spent a majority of the time contemplating how I could better the situation. Who could I ask for advice? What strategies haven't I tried? What could I do or say differently?

If you're a teacher reading this, I know you've had one of these moments, if not hundreds! It was a while before I finally stopped and realized how much time I spent thinking about these students who were not even my children! And, if I'm thinking about them this much, I know their parents are thinking of them a hundred times more. If parents and teachers would commit to combining their love and expertise for children, such an effort would not only help the children in school but in life. Unfortunately, it does not happen organically. For years, teachers and parents exist in analogous lives - both busy, hardworking, and determined yet hardly ever crossing paths. Our desire is to change students' lives because they have a "power team" of parents and teachers working behind them to help them succeed. We want to provide a guide for parents to use in the midst of their children's journey through school.

As soon as I had the idea, I called my mom to help. While I teach the "little ones" in kindergarten, she teaches the "big kids" (also known as teenagers). A large part of why I wanted to become a teacher was my mother. She is passionate about her students, and I have watched in awe as they pass through her classroom. The students admire and respect her, which is an accomplishment every teacher longs for. When I began teaching, my mom provided many answers to my concerns and questions. Having such an inspirational figure so close to me, I thought it would be an honor to have her co-write this book.

So, here we are, a mother-daughter team, sharing our perspectives and others' and hoping to create an unbeatable team for the students. Our lives are often misunderstood. As a teacher, we are constantly on display to students and parents even if we make mistakes, have bad days, or get overwhelmed. It is a difficult, challenging, and rewarding world but it is our passion. After discussing the content of the book, my mother and I decided that the most accurate way to share a teacher's perspective was to talk to as many teachers as possible. As a result we polled passionate teachers from all over the country to contribute. We asked one single question to each teacher and asked him or her to respond honestly to us:

"If you could give parents one piece of advice that would help their child succeed in the classroom what would it be?"

What we received was an overwhelming response of stories, concerns, and hopes from teachers who realize how important it is to work as a team with parents in order to benefit the students. No matter how different the story was, the underlying message was the same: teachers want their students to succeed and are willing to do whatever it takes to help students reach personal success. By personal success we mean the success that is deemed important to that student. For some it will be academic success, for others it will be developing social skills, and for others it might be communication skills. Regardless of how a student or a family defines success, teachers are in the business of helping students succeed. In the process of reading and hearing all of these stories and tips, we found ten "common themes" and from that the *Top 10 Things Teachers Want Parents to Know* was born. Therefore the title we chose, *Sincerely, The Teacher,* says it all; this is a collection of letters, stories, and advice from teachers all over the country written to you-the parent. In the following chapters you will find first-hand tips that teachers use daily that actually work. After all, it takes a lot of skill to keep the attention of 30 students for a long day of classes!

What you will find in this book are not only strategies that pertain to success in education but also strategies for life. The manners, behaviors, and rituals found in the classroom can also be carried into adulthood. As adults, we use many of the skills we learned in school at our jobs and in our relationships. No wonder there is that term, "I learned everything I need to know in kindergarten!" Starting in kindergarten, we learn how to listen, share, problem-solve, and maintain order. Most of these behaviors begin at home and are refined in the classroom as the child matures but, it starts with the parents *at home.*

This book has three main goals: to strengthen one of the most important and influential relationships available: the parent-teacher relationship, to provide an easy to read book for the busy parent, and to empower parents that they are the most influential individuals in their child's life.

Imagine what our future would look like if our nation's students had a bond of parents and teachers working together to ensure success in their future! In order to maximize the relationship, good teachers learn to value and embrace that relationship. We realize parents can feel out of place in their child's school especially if the parent had a bad experience while in school. Parents are also worried about entrusting their children to that brand new teacher or the teacher with the tough reputation. As one parent voiced, "[Teachers] spend more time with my children on a daily basis than I do! I am trusting them to take over when I cannot be there. That's a huge responsibility and one that I don't give away easily." While parents want to spend as much time as they can with their precious little ones (or big ones), children are required to go to school, someone must work to make a living, and someone needs to run the household - leaving *time* a rare commodity. As a result, parents have to trust that their children will be loved and cared for during those eight hours. The trust parents have for their children's teachers is huge.

"What you will find in this book are not only strategies that pertain to success in education but strategies for life."

You might be surprised to discover that because teachers know about this trust and the expectations parents have for them, teachers are just as concerned about their performances in the classroom. You will see in the following chapters that teachers are just as nervous to meet with you. In fact, next week just happens to be parent-teacher conferences at our school and my stomach already has butterflies! Like most teachers, I am excited yet nervous to meet with my students' parents.

Sincerely, The Teacher is designed for parents to hear first-hand tips from teachers. In turn you will gain an appreciation and understanding of our nation's teachers and hopefully trusting and working with them will become easier.

The second objective we had was designing this book for the busy parent. Everyday we see parents juggling their families, jobs and lives, so we understand that limited time is available for reading. We made an effort to keep this book easy-to-read and entertaining yet informative. As a kindergarten teacher, keeping the attention of twenty 5-year-olds I must be entertaining and informative. Let's face it, my mom has to do the same for her seniors in high school!

The ultimate and final goal of this book, however, is to empower you, the parent, to see that no matter who you are, where you live, what job you have, or what education you have, *you* are the most important factor in your child's education. *Parents are the key.*

Chapter 1

Graduation starts in Kindergarten

"Teachers are caring people who want to use their knowledge to get others ahead in life."
~High school senior

Foundations for a better tomorrow must be laid today. -Anonymous

One of the most delightful occasions that I have had the opportunity to observe was a kindergarten graduation. The ceremony was complete with diploma, tassels, and tiny blue caps and gowns. It was adorable! The five year olds in their caps and gowns were even more adorable as they raced to the stage and very solemnly accepted their diplomas while proud mamas and papas snapped countless pictures. The ceremony made a statement to the children and their families to encourage their accomplishments in education into their future. I thought to myself, "this is where is all begins." It was the beginning of their twelve-year journey in education.

Now, let's fast forward to my world in secondary education. Last night was graduation night at my high school. The final research paper has been turned in, the last homework assignment completed and the last prom danced for these seniors. Graduation is the final act of high school. These students are at the end of their twelve-year journey.

I must admit that as a faculty member, graduations are bittersweet evenings for me. I say goodbye to a group of students who I have had the pleasure to watch grow up. Each school day life unfolds in living color with these amazing teenagers. I am on the front lines as it all happens - whether it involves a romantic breakup, celebrating the relief that they scored well on their SAT exams, receiving the news they got into the college of their dreams, or dealing with the heaviness of the sudden death of a parent. Each of those scenarios played out this year. I will miss these seniors but college happens and it is time for these eagles to fly. Every spring when I say goodbye to another senior class it pulls at my heartstrings, but, for now, I am in the moment with them as they await their prize.

The time for the ceremony has arrived and the seniors are full of energy and excitement. They look so scholarly in their ceremonial caps and gowns. The traditional "mortarboard" (graduation caps) are angled at every direction on their heads and it makes me laugh. The girls are worried it makes their hair look flat and goofy. No matter what they look like, they are here and ready to graduate. The seniors have been talking about this moment all year. It is commonly known as "senioritis." They are ready to exit high school. Bring back any memories of your own graduation?

We are now gathering to celebrate this class and to reward all their wonderful accomplishments. It is heartwarming to watch the families and friends arrive at the ceremony all dressed up and excited to participate in this very special event in their children's lives. As their senior video proved, it was a very good year.

Adding to the joy of the evening, I am one of the faculty members assigned to the hallway with the graduating seniors. My duties suddenly begin when another faculty member comes running up to me and hands me a box of ties, informing me that I will "need" these. I look into the brown box jammed full of wrinkled, plaid, paisley, striped men's ties. It would have made Ralph Lauren cry. I really do not think I will need them; I assume that all the senior boys will have on a tie as instructed. I use every tie out of that box before the night is over! The ties are straightened and the appreciative young men are back in line in no time and ready for the cameras!

As the seniors are getting in line, the hallway becomes full of excitement and nervous anticipation. I can tell that their self-confidence is at an all time high. As I look over the sea of blue caps and gowns, I can't help but envision a future famous movie producer, a professional baseball player, or perhaps a future president of the United States. It is a moving experience to be in the presence of a future of possibilities.

The violins can be heard methodically beginning to play the traditional graduation march "Pomp and Circumstance" that's been performed since the early 1900's. The very sound of the melody has been sending chills up graduates' spines ever since. The seniors come to attention and quietly begin to file into the auditorium.

There is such a sense of pride and joy as each name is called and each senior receives a diploma. In unison they move their tassel, throw their hats in the air and it is over just like that! The hallways are quickly filled with families and friends. It is a beautiful, warm sight to see all the proud parents, cameras, flowers, and hugs waiting for each senior.

Empty seats in the auditorium

As I stand on duty in the hallway, I am reminded that there are seniors missing in that flurry of hats flying and Kodak moments. Along with all the joy I feel for all these accomplished graduating seniors, I am mindful of the seniors who did not walk across the stage that night. I want all seniors and their families to have the chance to experience the night that I am witnessing.

As I drive home from the evening's pomp and circumstance, I feel unsettled. Like my daughter, I think about things as I drive. It is quiet and I can think. I kept thinking: how could students with so much potential not graduate? What happened in that gap from those darling five year olds in their tiny caps and gowns to the senior who did not get to wear the cap and gown?

Across the nation, there are alarming statistics relating to high school graduation rates. We live in a time where on average only 7 out of every

10 American students graduate from high school. I am not going to dwell on the dismal data. It is obvious that the numbers of seniors not graduating across the nation is too high. The question is: how can we fix it?

Rock or sand?

We could talk about testing skills, staffing choices, curriculum changes, and use of cutting-edge technology in the classrooms. These are all critical areas where we need to strive for excellence; however, I am convinced that we need to go back to the beginning. We need to evaluate the foundation being built to prepare our students to learn. Successful students are the ones who desire knowledge and take pride in doing well in their schoolwork. This knowledge and pride stems only if a positive, consistent, and strong foundation is built from the beginning. Building the right foundation to influence children in this direction involves a plan on the part of the parents from kindergarten through high school. Parents have to be a part of the process for students to reach the graduation goal. I can't help but think of the famous parable of two men, one wise one foolish, whose homes depended upon the strength of the foundation. The wise man, of course, built his home on solid rock, so when the storms came and the wind blew his house remained intact. Unfortunately, the foolish man built his home on sand, so when the storms came and the wind blew, his house was washed away.

Parents want their children to have foundations built on rock but deliberate steps need to be taken in a child's life to build a solid foundation for her educational experience. Parents are the key to establishing this foundation. Then they need to continue to build upon the foundation for all twelve years of their child's schooling. What that foundation laying looks like will vary with each parent. What is important is that parents must have a plan to guide their child through the educational years.

Establish a love of learning

So, where do we start? The most important place to begin a child's educational experiences is in the home. Parents are their child's first teacher. Parents are the most significant influence on their child's attitude towards the educational process. Parents train their children to be taught long before the child is in a formal classroom setting. When children are very young they need direction in developing an interest for learning and acquiring knowledge. The foundation for positive learning is being built during this process. The parent is the developer and creator of this process. It will take time and energy, but the payoff is huge! Establishing the joy of learning is best done when the child is young, and yet it is never too late to begin even with an older student. When a child arrives in the classroom, the teacher-student experience will benefit tremendously as a result of the foundation that the parents have laid. Teachers do not build the foundation; parents do.

" Parents are their child's first teacher." "

As students begin to respond to learning, praise for discovering something new and encouragement for sharing that information, their educational foundation is being established. As they move toward school, parents need to help them respect the classroom environment and care about the educational experience; respect for education is critical for a child to learn. It will help them to "own" their time and work as a student. They must learn to value what they are doing in the classroom. As adults, we invest time and energy in those things that we deem valuable. Students need to see their education in the same context. It will help them to engage in the learning that takes place in their classrooms.

The chances are higher that high school students will still be engaged in their education if they have been operating in this manner since kindergarten. An engaged student is a successful student. My daughter commented that she could tell even with her 5 year olds which children have been trained to respect the classroom environment. In fact, one father e-mailed Tiffany the first week of school only to inform her that "Teaching is one of the most important yet underpaid professions available." He stated that"although this is kindergarten, I want my child to succeed in life and I know it starts here. Please let me know anything I can do to help my child succeed." This was a dad who got it!

Develop good habits early

The heart of a parent is for his child to excel in life. Excelling is defined differently in every family and differently for each student. We will not all produce the next Einstein or Michael Jordan, but we can help to shape students who can excel in an area of life. Education is an integral part of equipping the child to do just that. Students need a foundation of effective habits that will help them to get the most out of their education. As they move along and mature in their schooling, these habits adjust and change, but they are still a fundamental part of how the student functions in the classroom.

I have been both parent and teacher in the educational system. These roles have afforded me a chance to work side by side with dedicated parents and teachers. I have observed countless students and their educational habits. The students who have the most success in handling the classroom environment are students who maintain habits of organization, prioritization, curiosity, respect for others, and respect for self. These are habits that are learned on a day-to-day basis through interaction with others.

As you interact with your child, you might demonstrate what it looks like to be organized in your home. Clutter can oftentimes cause a person stress because it makes it challenging to stay on top of things like bills, important dates, and documents. Explain to your child why it is important to be organized for them, too. If he is organized at school, then he will have a much easier time keeping up with homework and project due dates. Establish a mindset where you begin with the end in mind. This is your child's beginning. This is the time to instill habits in your children that count.

Position your child for sucess

Like coaches who work with their players to train them to get into position to make certain plays, parents position their children to be successful in the classroom. They put attitudes, habits, practices, and expectations in motion that will be the "plays" that their child uses in school. Parents can coach their children to have fun learning all their lives and to value education.

I am very practical in my approach to teaching. In my high school classes, I want my students to walk out of my class into life with tools to help them handle life's situations. It is also vital that parents develop in their children a positive mindset toward education long before the teacher ever receives them in their classroom. Incorporate these things into your daily flow of life. Having a plan established in your home will set your child in position to be successful. Your child's future teachers will be ever grateful for your hard work and dedication. Your child will be grateful.

Recently I heard a doctor take a moment to introduce his mother. He then stopped and said that he would not be where he was today if it were not for his mom. He said that she continually used flashcards, checked out library books and established homework routines as he went through school. He thanked her in front of everyone for the educational foundation she laid for him. Patients in the ER would like to thank her too, I'm sure.

Our hope is that your child will be thanking you one day as well. In order to achieve that goal here are 10 guidelines that educators saw as important in laying a foundation for your children (many of which we will cover in detail in later chapters).

10 Guidelines for Setting a Positive Foundation for Your Child

1. *Be a living example of learning to your child.* The love of learning is developed early in a child's life. The best way to enhance your child's curiosity towards life is to model it yourself. Make the time to take an on-line course, read an educational book on an interesting subject, or try a new recipe on the food network channel. Show your child that you are never "too old" to learn. Learning is a life-long adventure. Model your desire to learn for your child as they are going through school. I remember the numerous questions my daughters would ask me when they were young, "Why is the sky blue? Why can't we fly?" These questions are great examples of curiosity and you should be proud of your children for being so inquisitive. I also know that parents, like me, don't always know the answers to our little one's questions; so model how to find the answers on the Internet, in a book, or at the library.

2. *Speak positively about education and "getting to go" to school.* A child will quickly pick up on your positive attitude towards the opportunity of education and will embrace it. The actual words that you use when speaking about school, learning, teachers, etc. are very powerful. Be careful what you say. Positive attitudes cultivate good attitudes towards school. Negative and critical attitudes do just the opposite.

3. *Plan educational activities for your family.* For family night, watch a program on the History channel, Animal Planet or HGTV (one of my favorites). Plan outings to a museum, visit historical sights in your area, develop a family book club, or just be creative and search your local area for opportunities for learning. One of the restaurants near me even started offering cooking classes. Most cities are improving their efforts to provide free, educational activities for families. It often just takes a little time looking online or in the local newspaper to find educational events near you.

4. *Make learning and the idea of school FUN!* I have always been a believer that learning is and must include fun! I have proven that maxim many times in my classroom. Of course, there are those serious instructional lessons, but fun instructional lessons need to be in the mix. However, as a parent you have the independence to do educational activities that your child enjoys. If your child loves dinosaurs, for example, be on the lookout for any exhibits, movies, or books that involve dinosaurs. After the fact, your child can draw a picture of his favorite part and even write a sentence about it.

5. *Train your child to have the disciplines of stillness and listening to instruction.* In this day and age of the electronic media our children are conditioned to be entertained in order to keep their attention. Some days I feel like I need to bring in monkeys and elephants to keep students' attention! Even the smallest of children can be trained to be good listeners. The best way to teach this skill is to practice it. Encourage your child to stay focused on one activity at a time. Some activities that will enhance this skill in children are listening to books on tape or attending plays, museums, and church services. Practicing the disciplines of listening and stillness will make it more comfortable for the child in the classroom setting.

6. *Look for teachable moments in your everyday life.* You are your child's first teacher. Never feel intimidated that you are not smart enough or cannot handle the title of "teacher." All that you do with your child is a teaching opportunity. Your conversations, walks in the park, grocery shopping, and your daily life is a wonderful time to teach, train, and instruct your precious child. Look at every opportunity as a chance to teach something new to your child, whether it is about education, about life, or about relationships.

7. *Think out of the box when it comes to the education of your child.* As one of my former principals said, "Do whatever it takes to make learning happen." Be creative in your approach to whatever you are doing with your child. You might be surprised how well your child responds to a challenge. For example, count beans, M&M's, or gumdrops to teach math. Play games in the car as you travel. Have your children watch signs along the road to come up with all the letters in the alphabet or spell a certain word.

8. *Establish respect for authority*. Growing up southern, my girls were trained to say, "Yes" not "Yeah" when talking to adults. It is a small act but it reinforces the fact that adults are different than peers. Respect for authority is practiced throughout a person's entire life, so learning it early is imperative. Teach your children to address adults respectively by looking them in the eyes when speaking to them and not to interrupt. It is a skill that we as adults use in the working world as well.

9. *Establish priorities.* Even as adults we struggle with prioritizing and time management. I always used to tell my girls, "Do your have-to's first and your want-to's last." Learning the differences between "have-to's" and "want-to's" is a great foundation builder for children. You can do this by teaching your child how to make a "to do" list and share yours. Talk openly about your want-to's and how to achieve them. For example, "I want to go on a vacation to the beach, so I have to first work hard to earn the money, plan the trip, and then prepare to go." Being open with the process helps establish a sense of priorities and it helps show your children that vacations just don't happen.

10. *Practice problem solving.* The classroom is full of students who come from a multitude of backgrounds and who have different personalities. It is safe to say that eventually your child will face a problem. If you have already established a problem solving strategy at home, it will alleviate a lot of stress later. Your family's strategy can be unique to you. There are also many resources available online that can be used or printed out to work as visual reminders of how to problem solve. Research what works best for your personalities and beliefs. This is your family, and you are your family's expert.

Each of these ten steps should be implemented in some fashion all twelve years of school. It takes a resolve on the part of the parents to make this part of their daily routine. Teachers need the parent's help before we receive them in our classrooms. It enhances the ability of the teacher in teaching children at any age.

It is a new school year. When I was leaving school today, one of my students ran up to me to show me the shirt and tie for his senior pictures. He wanted me to vote. "Which shirt would look tight (that means cool)?" I gave him my vote but said that either would look really nice. He is a fine young gentlemen and a leader in the senior class. Here I go again, another school year, another class to get to know and appreciate. But I am not going there yet. I have some great memories to make ahead of me this year and lots of laughing and fun learning!

You choose the cycle

"A teacher makes you smart. They help you if you can't open
something."
~Kindergarten student

In school we learn several different types of cycles. There is the butterfly life cycle where a tiny egg turns into caterpillar, then into a cocoon,
and finally into a beautiful butterfly. The butterfly then creates another
egg starting the cycle all over again. We learn about the water cycle
where water starts out in rivers, lakes, and oceans and then evaporates
into the atmosphere. The water droplets form clouds, which get heavy
and eventually produce rain to fall back into the rivers, lakes, and
oceans. Life is full of cycles. It is a natural, wonderful phenomenon of
nature.

What many might not know is there is also a cycle that involves your
child's home and school environment. What parents say and do at home
can determine how a child performs and behaves at school. In return,
whatever happens at school can greatly affect what happens at home.
Eventually it becomes a cycle. This relationship can be good news or
bad news depending on the cycle. If parents and teachers want to work
together the appropriate cycle has to be in place. It is not always easy
but like any relationship it takes effort, and the effort is definitely worth

it. It is called the "Home and School Cycle" of which there are two forms: The Positive Home to School / School to Home Cycle

> "What parents do and say at home can determine how a child performs and behaves at school."

a Negative Home to School / School to Home Cycle. The descriptions may be simple but the results are all too real and often have an immense impact on your child's life.

The Positive Home to School Cycle

The Positive Home to School Cycle is initiated when parents speak positively about their child's teacher, school, or administration outside of the school setting. The words can be as simple as phrases like:

- *"That was such a neat activity your class did. Your teacher is very creative."*
- *"I talked to your teacher today and I can tell she cares a lot about you and your friends."*
- *"I am so glad you have Mrs. Smith as your teacher this year."*

It might seem unimportant but the child is hearing words that are respectful, uplifting, and honoring about his teacher. As the parents model these words of affirmation, the child takes in their words and the tone in which they are said. In return, the child is more likely to also respect and honor the teacher and school environment. Many psychologists would call this action *positive priming*. Though it often occurs unconsciously, priming gets us ready to notice certain things and to feel and act in certain ways. Sometimes priming people with only a few words can make a difference in their behavior, both positive or negative.

Just a few affirmative words can have a positive affect on your child's school environment, but you might not see a change in your child's behavior immediately. The goal is to just get them thinking positively about school. Over time, the positive priming will position the student to respect his teacher. When students respect teachers they are more likely to perform well and thrive, and the teacher gets to see respectful students. When a student respects me as an adult, as well as the school, it uplifts and encourages me as a teacher. I then feel energized and encouraged to be a better teacher. As a result, it is even easier for the student and parent to respect and honor me because I am working with boosted energy and encouragement. As you can see a few simple words can be the start of a wonderful, positive Home to School Cycle.

I was blessed my first year of teaching to have a wonderful group of parents who encouraged and worked with me for the well-being of their children. It was their kind words that helped me to strive to become a better teacher. I wanted to fulfill their expectations as I helped guide their precious little ones through life. One mother truly stands out in my mind when thinking of the Positive Home to School Cycle. Every time she came into the classroom she never failed to speak an uplifting word. She often talked about how she "was telling a friend," or "talking with some other moms from the class" about our classroom, me as a teacher, or how happy she was with our classroom. She did not go on and on. She spoke just a few simple, sweet words; the compliments brightened up my day and urged me to meet her expectations. Her daughter was a wonderful indicator of her mother's words. The little girl was nothing but honoring, respectful, and helpful, and I know it had a lot to do with what the mom was saying at home.

The Positive School to Home Cycle

The reverse cycle, the School to Home Cycle, works in a similar manner. When your child is blessed with a teacher who is positive, encouraging, and loving you will see a change in the child's behavior at home. You might notice behaviors such as:

- Increased confidence
- Motivation
- Eagerness to please
- Respect for authority
- Responsibility

The change in behavior might not be immediate, but if the teacher is modeling, practicing, and requiring actions like the ones above, it is more likely that they will be repeated at home. Soon they might even become a habit! If your child is blessed to have an uplifting teacher, don't be afraid to say something. Giving the teacher a compliment will only encourage her to continue the behavior. One parent stated, "When I could tell that the teacher and I were on the same page, wanting the same things for my child, I could be a better parent and she could be a better teacher - teamwork but in separate settings." Teachers and parents both want the best for the children but we need each other's help. Parents are looking for someone to guide and love their child when they are not present, and teachers need support, encouragement, and information from parents in order to do our jobs to the best of our ability.

The Negative Home to School Cycle

The Negative Home to School Cycle is usually sparked by several factors such as miscommunication, differing viewpoints, and student performance in academics. Every parent will face at least one of the above factors at least once in their child's school career, but it is how the parents handle the situation that causes the negative cycle. When parents do not agree with the teacher it is easy to be vocal about how much they do not agree with or respect the decision being made. If the child is present during the vocalization, what he may hear can be negative and belittling talk about his teacher and school. If the situation does not get resolved and the vocalizing continues, then more than likely the child will assume his parents' frustrations and negative feelings. Remember, young children especially tend to mimic those around them and they want to please their authority figures. Children will repeat and model what is done at home.

Similarly to the positive priming I mentioned earlier in the chapter, children can also be primed with negative words. If someone says some very rude words to you, on most occasions it will affect your mood and behavior negatively. Even though the parent's words might be few, they have a big impact. As a result if a student hears disrespectful words about a teacher at home it will mostly likely cause disrespect in the classroom and very possibly disobedient acts. When children do not respect their teacher and school, it is very difficult to perform to their highest potential and thrive.

The teacher is another person to consider in the negative cycle. When a student and/or parent spouts negative talk and demonstrates an obvious sense of disrespect toward the teacher or her decision, the teacher suffers. A lot of energy is expended on the part of the defensive teacher who must constantly be defending his actions and words. Teachers receiving constant negative feedback will feel discouraged, may be hurt, and exhausted. Unfortunately, once that the teacher is weary and discouraged, it makes it easier for parents to talk negatively of her again. The teacher has begun to live out the negative script written for her by the parents. It isn't hard to see that a few negative words can eventually stem into the unwanted negative cycle.

The Negative School to Home Cycle

One year your child might be placed with a teacher who is negative, uses harsh words, has unrealistic expectations, or there is just a miss-match of personalities between the teacher and child. Many are familiar with the story of world-renown Olympic swimmer, Michael Phelps. His mother openly shares the story of a teacher who informed her that she believed Michael would never be able to focus on anything. Apparently what the teacher saw was someone who was active and easily distracted. What the teacher missed was that when encouraged and placed in the right environment, Michael was very focused and used his activeness for a positive outcome. If your child faces a similar challenging environment, then over time it could affect your child at home. Oftentimes the child might become:

- Frustrated
- Unmotivated
- Short-tempered
- Insecure
- Self-doubtful

The behaviors could be internalized or very apparent depending on the child and situation. The best thing a parent can do is talk to the child openly about the subject. Ask questions and let her know that it is okay to share. Watch for temperament changes in your child and try to determine the source. Your child may not be able to verbalize that he feels incapable of the tasks. But you can ask him what do others say about him; how is the teacher when working one-on-one? Impatience may not be a behavior he can say, but he may be able to describe how the teacher taps her foot or rolls her eyes when he is talking to her. If there is an issue, listen to the facts from your child; yet wait to discuss it with the teacher to hear her side of the story as well. After hearing both sides, a rational, unemotional opinion can be made, and you can choose what to say to your child about the situation and give him direction as to how he should respond to the teacher.

Since your child's education is a 12-year journey, expect that there will be at least one teacher who creates what my mom likes to call, "a sandpaper relationship." A sandpaper relationship is when communication and interaction with another person constantly feels rough and rigid. Don't let this discourage you because it would not be real life if everybody got along and agreed on every subject. Controlled and careful confrontation helps shape us as individuals. How else would you feel truly passionate about your beliefs unless someone challenged you? Embrace the sandpaper relationship as a learning experience for you and your child. Some day your children will have to learn that there are people out there who will challenge and test them; why not help walk them through it? Show your child that she can still maintain respect for someone's position while also communicating with the person about any issues at hand.

Oftentimes this means that you need to schedule a time to talk with your child's teacher. By no means go in with fists up ready for a fight. Instead, communicate in an open, unassuming manner. Wait until the steam has evaporated before you confront the teacher. A good night's sleep may give you enough perspective and patience to discuss the situation in a calm and caring manner. The goal is change – in your child or the teacher's behavior. Making an appointment and sitting down with the teacher may allow the two of you to resolve the situation together.

Also talk to your child's teacher first *before* involving the administration. The teacher is the direct line to your child not the administration. If you feel there is a problem with the teacher do not call the principal. Call the teacher first and give her the chance to discuss the concerns with you. Going over the head of the teacher may only cause more animosity later on.

How to Avoid a Negative Cycle

As a disclaimer, I am not suggesting to blindly agree with all of your child's teachers. As in every profession, teaching is not exempt from having those few who have their own agenda or have lost their passion. There might definitely be an issue that needs to be addressed. The main point is that how you handle the situation will result in either a negative or positive cycle. In order to avoid a negative cycle I have included some tips.

Give grace where it is needed

Oftentimes the Negative Home to School Cycle occurs after the teacher makes a mistake. No matter how hard teachers try, mistakes happen. Papers get lost here or there, something gets graded incorrectly, or the wrong thing is said. In every profession, we all have our days. Family emergencies come up, sickness strikes, or exhaustion takes over. Of course, if it becomes a habit then it needs to be addressed; however, sometimes the best remedy is grace. It meant so much to me when after making a mistake a parent would simply say, "It is okay. I understand." So many times parents do understand, and when they respond in that way it takes a weight off of my shoulders and I can concentrate on fixing the mistake I made (and hopefully not doing it again). The vice versa is definitely true for teachers. Oftentimes teachers just need to give grace to parents who are busy, forget a meeting, or don't send in a promised item. We are in this together, so let's give each other the benefit of a doubt.

Watch what you say.

Most parents have learned the hard way that it is always best to be cautious about what you do and say around others. A humorous quote by an anonymous author states, "Children seldom misquote you. In fact, they usually repeat word for word what you shouldn't have said." Although very true, there are times when even the most careful of parents can be misunderstood by their precious little ones.

Both parents and teachers must realize that what students say might not always be exact. Although students often bring home great tales about school, there is always a chance for a misunderstanding. Teachers are not always mad and students are not always unruly. Ask specific questions: why do you think Mrs. Smith was mad today? You might find out that Johnny dropped the desk on her foot and she had to leave school because it was broken. Yes, she had tears in her eyes, but so would all of us.

"Children seldom misquote you. In fact, they usually repeat word for word what you shouldn't have said."

Children are quite literal beings, and even the most careful of parents can say words that children misunderstand. That crazy teacher may actually be a compliment as in "I can't believe that crazy teacher loves that classroom of runny noses and sticky fingers." As long as parents and teachers can refrain from making an immediate judgment, once an explanation is given from either party, the answer is usually quite simple. One teacher we found starts each year telling the parents jokingly, "I won't believe everything the students tell me at school, if you will do the same at home."

In order to benefit the students, teachers and parents must be careful with our words, slow to make a judgment, and patient if there is a misunderstanding. Allowing room for open communication is the best remedy for a miscommunication. Not only is it wise to be cautious with words spoken to your child, it is even wise to be cautious in your words with a friend or a spouse. If I've learned anything in my years teaching, it is that there are always little ears around no matter if we see them or not.

The summer before I began teaching I worked as a nanny for two small girls. Since it was summer, we spent most of the days at the pool or at swim team. I vividly remember one of my first times at swim team practice. I was standing by some mothers who were talking about the local school. They began talking about how much they disliked the principal and then eventually the teachers. The moms were very verbal in their complaints, as well as the gossip they had heard. There were a lot of moms contributing to the conversation and even more listening. If a mom did not know about the teacher, she sure did after that conversation! They talked about the teachers to have as well as the teachers to avoid. Then I heard, "I don't want Ms. Smith because she's fresh out of college and won't have a clue what's going on." These last words especially broke my heart because *I* was about to be that new teacher. After hearing those words, I immediately assumed no one would want me as a teacher.

I share this story to emphasize how important it is to be watchful of what you say about your child's school and teachers wherever you are. Not only did I hear those hurtful words but several moms and students who were not participating in the educational bashing heard them as well. It made me rethink whether I truly wanted to become a teacher or not. I'm glad I did eventually become a teacher, but it took some toughing up to realize that not everyone will like me and speak complimentarily about me all of the time. That is why the mother's words I mentioned earlier meant so much to me. When she said that she was talking about me in a good way in another setting, it meant the world to me. Words hurt and affect whoever hears them, whether it is a child or a future teacher. That's why it is best to just be careful.

Parents want the best for their child, especially when it comes to the teacher who will be in their child's life for the next year. However, giving your child's teacher the benefit of a doubt is not only helpful to you as a parent but to your child as well. Compared to other parents, all parents have a different experience with their child's teacher. Some parents may love the teacher while some may not. It is important to be cautious about what you listen to because no parent wants to willingly confess that her child is a challenge in school; so, what you might be hearing is a jaded version. Choose to start each school year with a clean slate and make your own relationship with the teacher.

Be realistic

Being realistic about your child's strengths and weaknesses is one of the best gifts you can give your child and her teacher. Another cause and the most likely culprit of the Negative Home to School Cycle is the

"Choose to start each school year with a clean slate and make your own relationship with the teacher."

introduction of bad news. Oftentimes teachers have to be the bearer of bad news. We are trained to identify signs that could result in possible behavior problems, learning disabilities, and developmental issues. It is our job to make parents aware of any concerns or observations we have. Teachers can get in grave legal trouble if they ignore a sign and do not contact a parent. This is one of my least favorite jobs as a teacher. It is not fun to have to tell parents news that they do not want to hear. Even though it is not an easy task to tell parents news like this, if both the teacher and parent remember that the child has many more positive qualities than negative qualities then it makes the issue a lot easier to discuss.

One parent states, "Parents need to be honest about their children's limitations and struggles as much as they are about their strengths and gifts. Making a little god out of your child does not benefit the child, or the parent, or the teacher. Teachers need to deal honestly with parents, but gently and in a teamwork sort of way, while parents need to be 'teachable' about their children and accept the counsel and wisdom of the teacher when there is a problem. It needs to work both ways, each respecting the others' role." Each child has strengths and weaknesses.

To be open and accepting that children will have both strengths and weaknesses is not only helpful for your child but also helpful for you and your child's teacher. Just because your child is struggling in a part of school does not make you a bad parent. It means your child is a human being, and that is okay. Usually the reason teachers inform parents when there is a struggle is because they are coming to you to ask what you can do together to help your child. They need your help because you are the parent. You know this child the best and your insight and time can help immensely. You can help your child by helping the teacher, by being a team even when the news is not what you expected for your young Einstein (who, by the way, had tremendous learning challenges but managed to make a name for himself anyway)!

Choose your own cycle

It does not matter if you come from a family of Harvard grads or from a family of high school dropouts, you get to choose the cycle that your family experiences. The words and encouragement that you give can change your child's education. If you would like to break the negative cycle set in place by your past, you can.

One of my favorite inspirational stories is about a young girl from Mississippi. From a very young age the girl moved from multiple houses and faced abuse from various family members. It was not until she was a teenager that she was able to move in with her father. Despite his stern and caring nature, the girl still struggled with rebellious behaviors. Her father remained loving, yet strict and eventually her behavior turned around. Her father's high expectations and encouragement later allowed her to pursue her passion for media and journalism. She eventually graduated with honors and landed a job as a news anchor for a television program in Nashville. It was when she moved to Chicago to host an early morning talk show that her career began to kick off. The ratings for the talk show skyrocketed as people fell in love with her personality and opinions on life. Within a year the talk show was renamed, "The Oprah Winfrey Show," after this amazing young woman. Today millions of people all over the world have been influenced and inspired by Oprah. Her story is a wonderful example of a cycle that started off negatively but with love and encouragement was transformed into a positive one.

The choice is yours. Which cycle will you choose? All it takes is a choice, and the cycle, whichever you choose, will begin.

Chapter

3

We are all on the same team

"A teacher is someone who impacts those around them, inspires students, and is always willing to listen to others' views as well as stand strong on their own."
~High school student

"Coming together is a beginning, staying together is progress, and working together is success." Henry Ford

High school sports events have an energy all their own. During the school year I make it a practice to support my student athletes by attending their events. Each fall brings a new football season with renewed enthusiasm. On game night, I typically grab an extra pair of gloves, a blanket, and head out the door to get a stadium seat. As I near the stadium I can see the glow of the "Friday night lights" just over the treetops. If I roll my window down, I can hear the beat of our amazing drum line. One of the members of the band is in my homeroom, and I often tell him that the football games would not be the same without the band. Once inside the stadium, the school spirit electrifies the air with the sound of the cheering fans, the rhythm of the band, and the chants lead by the cheerleaders. It is school pride and community at its best.

Our football team made it to the playoffs one particular year and the night of the big game I decided to sit with the parents of players who were in my classes. As the game played out, the score became very close. We needed a win to advance to the playoffs. Our section became very enthusiastic and loud as we cheered on the team. A relative of one of the players leaned over to me at one point and asked me which player belonged to me. Without hesitation I answered "all of them." She laughed and said, "Oh, you must be a teacher."

" Teachers are an extension of the parents."

I must admit that I felt a sense of ownership and a mother's pride as I claimed them all as mine. It was at that moment that I realized the significance of the parent-teacher bond. We all share a strong comradery for the students on the field. We all share the desire to see their dreams come true of winning a playoff game and going "to the Dome." We all want their lives to be successful in whatever path they choose. This same sense of unity goes beyond the playing field at a Friday night football game and extends into each classroom Monday through Friday all school year long. Teachers are an extension of the parents. (By the way, our team made it to the third round of the playoffs-the "elite eight;" we were all so proud of them)!

In a sports team it is important for the members to know their role. The players cannot call all of the plays just like the coaches cannot jump onto the field and play. The sports team consists of the owners, coaches, fans, and players. All have a profound and specific roll to play in the experience of the sports player. It may not appear so at first but the school environment is similar to that of a sports team. The "educational team," which is made up of administrators, teachers, parents, and students, are also profound in the educational experience of each student. Both set of members need to have a team concept mindset, as well as grasp the importance of functioning as a partnership. In order to function in a partnership you must know your role, which is why we will spend this chapter illustrating what your role looks like in your child's school journey.

The Educational Team

In the educational setting, teamwork must be developed and implemented to bring about success. Each member has a specific role to play. In the *classroom setting* the owners are the administrators, teachers are the coaches, the parents are the fans, and the students are the players. The administrators are the ones looking at the big picture and making key decisions. Teachers are the professionals in their particular subject. Many years in college and graduate school have prepared them to be the expert in their field. Parents are the key adults in the life of the student. They cheer on, encourage, and guide their children in their educational paths. Parents are also the providers for whatever their child needs while in school. Students are the players doing the work. It is important for students to learn early on in their education to take ownership of what kind of work they will perform. It is our hope that they will choose to be students of excellence, which will carry over into their adult life to be men and women of excellence in all areas of their life.

The Owners

Administrators function like the owners of a sport's team. They look at the overall picture and make the big decisions. The Board of Education works with administrators in establishing policy for an entire school district. The administrators are the leaders of the educational team as they direct, implement, and establish school policy. They are responsible for creating guidelines and policy for all grade levels.

Data drives our educational system in the United States, just like data drives team owners to make decisions of who to keep, fire, or pay more. In our school building there are bar graphs displayed on the walls indicating the scores in math, science, and so on. These are visual reminders informing us of our performances in subjects. Individuals are hired for the sole purpose of analyzing and collecting data relating to student performance. With this data in hand, the leaders focus on adopting strategies that will help improve areas that are showing low performance. "Standards-based classrooms" are one such effort. Every teacher in the district must comply with the standards being set by the state and county for each subject taught. The decisions made by the administrators are designed to create success for all members of the educational team.

The Coaches

The teachers are the "coaches" of the educational team. They are on the field with the students (players) demonstrating, modeling, and directing the plays. They need to do whatever they can to make learning happen. Every classroom will reflect the personality and style of the teacher. Each teacher has her strengths and needs to emphasize those in the classroom. Just like the temperament, beliefs, and personality of a coach shapes a team; the temperament, beliefs, and personality of a teacher shapes the classroom.

Teachers are dedicated to helping their students become critical thinkers, so they share their knowledge with their students. Learning how to think independently will aid them throughout their lives. Enthusiasm and love for their subject may look differently classroom to classroom, but most teachers teach because of a high dedication and love of the subject. Teachers spend endless hours going over their "playbook" of creative ideas to present their subject matter to their students. They are relentless in their effort to explain their subject matter in an interesting manner to their students. Teachers are well aware of the fact that a student engaged in the classroom is a student who is learning. Teachers are taught how to diversify their lessons so that all types of students can comprehend the lesson being taught. Teachers want success in their classroom and that is accomplished by students understanding the "plays."

The Fans

No game is complete without the fans. Fans build the morale of the team. They encourage, they support, and they give the players a reason to play. In the classroom setting, parents are the "fans" and remain the ever-present support and advocate for the child. Students need their parents to be involved and interested in what they are doing in the classroom. They long for their parent's approval and want to make them proud. How often have you heard the phrase, "Mom, Dad watch this!"? Children constantly look to their parents for approval. Fortunately this lasts from the time your child is playing in the sandbox to when they're walking across the stage at graduation. The encouragement and support that comes from the parent is irreplaceable.

I love to watch the parents, especially the dads, during a sporting event. From their words and expressions, it is clear that many of them may have a "better" way to coach their children. Yet, they understand that their roles have changed and they must remain supportive. Parents can provide their child with whatever they need to make learning happen. Notice, they can provide – tools, supplies, words of encouragement but they are not to *do for* the child.

Parents know their child the best and in turn they can offer to assist an educator with teaching their child. I know from personal experience how helpful it is when a parent explains a particular detail about their child. I can make the adjustments I need to make for the good of that student. Children have what I like to call a "bend" in their personalities and abilities. This "bend" refers to one's naturally giftedness. Knowing their strengths will assist parents (and teachers) in guiding students in the appropriate direction to develop those skills and talents. Parents are their child's #1 cheerleader and fan.

However, parents are unique in the educational team because they play multiple roles. In the classroom setting parents are the fans but once school is out parents become the coaches too. If your child plays baseball you might spend time *outside* of games throwing the ball, giving tips, and watching pros on TV. Similarly, your time outside of school can be spent learning, reading, writing, and practicing the skills learned in the classroom. As you can see parents are key components in the educational team, and without them the team suffers.

The Players

The student is the "player" on this educational team. They are learning the plays and doing the work to carry out the desired result. Students need to learn how to take ownership of their role in their education and understand their position as students. Students need to develop a hard working and diligent approach to their schoolwork. Parents can equip their children from the very beginning of their education with these skills. Each child will have his own style and way of learning. As a teacher, I find it fascinating and fun to observe all the different ways students approach their schoolwork and learning. However, one thing is consistent with all students and that is that they take responsibility for the effort they put into their school work. Parents are teaching their children a wonderful life skill when they train them to take ownership and responsibility for their schooling. Real life will require this of your child in many areas of life, which why it is so crucial to have a team concept between all members of the educational team.

Team Concept between Parents and Teachers

From the first day of school, it is essential to start adopting a team concept between parents and teachers. Both are cheering on the student. Students who walk through the doors of our schools have a network of teachers wanting them to reach their greatest potential. Teachers want to be viewed by the parents as the student's advocate not adversary. As one of the other adult voices in the student's life teachers can be very influential. Therefore the teacher and parent need to move in unison as they navigate through the school year.

As I mentioned earlier, every teacher has his or her own personality and style of teaching just as some coaches throw chairs on the court (a la Bobby Knight) or pace the sidelines like Bear Bryant. The diversity of teaching styles is one of the challenges for students to discover. Every new school year students discover new teachers, new ways of doing school, and new challenges. Wise parents help their children adjust, adapt, and discover the differences between teachers. Real life will continually bring people in to their lives who they don't understand. Since your children are still school-age it is a great time to learn how to handle different kinds of people. When parents keep the team concept in mind as they get to know a teacher, everyone involved will benefit. Teamwork affords the opportunity to discover the value of diversity. It is yet another life skill to train students in getting along with different kinds of people.

Teachers work endlessly to create excellence in their classroom. As the instructional part of the year progresses, they give valuable input to the parents regarding their child's performance in the classroom. It is specific so that the parent can know specific strengths and weaknesses. Parents with a team concept in mind will receive even negative feedback as information that will assist them in isolating the needs of their child. Teachers hope that parents do not receive negative information as an attack on their parenting skills but rather as information to help redirect the child. Ultimately parents can then work more specifically with their children in the areas that they are having difficulties. As the parent and teacher work together, the child can learn the necessary skills to achieve success in the classroom environment. Team concept thinking has less drama and yields more concrete results. After all, we are partners in helping the students be successful – we are all cheering for the students!

A Vital Partnership

Teachers value and cherish support from parents. We need and cherish our parental support! As a parent, I know how much I treasured my daughters' teachers. They gave me invaluable insight about my children that I might have missed. A partnership goes beyond the idea of the team concept to the actual concept of backing each other up. The teacher and the parent work together for the good of the children to hold them accountable for their actions and their academic effort. There will be no throwing anyone under the bus here; we are allies in holding the students accountable and helping them to reach their potential. Support from our parents provides teachers the opportunity to be more effective in the classroom. It helps our leverage with a student if the child knows the parents are backing up the teacher. I cannot tell you how much I appreciate a parent who will stand behind me when a student has not completed her work. It is like a breath of fresh air! Even the best of students will come up with very creative "stories" to justify their incomplete work. It is best for the student if the parents do not make excuses when the student has fallen short of her task. When the parent has the expectation of honesty and accountability, it works wonders with students and is for their best interest.

"Support from our parents provides teachers the opportunity to be more effective in the classroom."

I value the open, honest, and transparent communication I have with parents. It keeps the student on their toes. One parent commented that whether public or private school, the key to her child's success was her OWN involvement in the school and with the teachers. Parents do not just pay a teacher to teach their child, they partner with the teacher in the child's educational journey as they encourage their children to take personal ownership and responsibility for the work required. When the child stumbles, they pick him up and cheer him forward; when the child "scores," they cheer him on.

Communicating with Kindness

Being in a partnership means that parents and teachers understand the importance of setting a good example in how we interact. The students are watching the adults and how they handle situations. They listen to the verbal exchanges and read the notes. It is crucial that we as adults watch what we say and remember that we are on the same side. Remember, as Tiffany mentioned in the previous chapter, you must choose the cycle. We all want what is best for the student even if hard facts need to be faced.

It is unpleasant for a teacher to tell parents something negative about their student whether it involves poor behavior or academic achievement. I have yet to meet anyone who enjoys getting bad news about anything. When it involves a child, it seems to be even more intense and tender. Successful teachers and parents realize that specific issues need to be addressed for the success of the child. Forgive those teachers who do not have excellent people skills when unfolding unpleasant things. Doctors face the same dilemma. Some have good bedside manners and some do not. But that rambling doctor may be the best cancer specialist in the medical field. That blunt teacher may have the skills and experience to help your child overcome an obstacle and soar.

Partnership and team concept thinking will not take the negative information and begin blaming, making excuses, or becoming defensive. Instead, the information becomes a fact that must be handled. The adult team goes to work to come up with a plan for the student to follow. It is always our hope that a student will make the necessary adjustments to fulfill the requirements of the class. If he chooses not to follow the plan, the teacher must grade him accordingly and parents may decide any other consequences.

School is about choices

Students make choices regarding their schoolwork from kindergarten to senior year in high school. The older they become, the more choices they make and the more factors are present to influence their choices. In the school setting, the child is learning lifelong lessons of respect, humility, self-discipline, and hard work. It is healthy to keep the children accountable for their choices. When they are forced to own their decisions, it contributes to their character development.

Teachers and parents especially need to lean on their partnership when a student is not making the best choices. They are the adult part of the team in the scenario and must function accordingly. Many factors influence a student's behavior on a given day. As a result, the teacher sees students in a different context than the parents, so as parents it is vital to keep an open mind and take note of what the teacher is observing. It is also very important that parents inform the teachers of anything that is going on in their home that may effect how their child is performing or behaving in school. The school system does not intend to pry or expect a family to reveal private information but a parent does help us do a better job instructing and placing expectations on the child if we are made aware of a situation. Parents and teachers are on the same team. Both want the student to succeed and do well.

It was incredible to be able to watch our team advance toward the state finals; being a part of a group working toward a goal builds community and focus. At times it was fun and sometimes it was just hard work for those boys to play in the rain against boys faster and larger. But, like school, the pay off is huge if we all stay in the game and give it our best.

10 Ways to Practice Teamwork.

1. *If your child makes an unwise choice at school, there needs to be a consequence at home.* Even if your child suffers a consequence at school for the action, don't let it stop there. Children need to see that there is a connection between home and school. Decide on a consequence for misbehavior at school and stick to it. Just saying, "Don't do that again," is not enough. Teachers need your support so the child understands that you are working together.

2. *View the teacher as your child's advocate.* The teacher is for your child and wants to see her succeed just as you do. Having this positive view of your child's teacher will help avoid future miscommunications.

3. *Be supportive of your child's teacher and their expectations.* Teachers design guidelines for the good of the entire class. Teachers set classroom expectations that fit their teaching style. Work with your child as you learn and understand the new guidelines each year. You may be surprised which expectations actually work and fit your child.

4. *Set a good example when speaking about a teacher.* Be a positive parent who influences your child in the same direction. A positive teacher, parent, and student team is a successful team. Choose your cycle.

5. *Inform teachers of issues occurring outside of school that may influence a child's disposition or performance.* The teacher will be able to understand better and make adjustments for your child if she knows about things like family illnesses, divorces, and vacations.

6. *Keep your child accountable.* Parents are the key to keeping students accountable for their choices. It is important for students to be aware that the adults in their life have expectations and guidelines for them to follow. It is imperative that they realize that mom and dad are in agreement with the teacher regarding accountability and responsibility.

7. *Do little things that will encourage the teacher.* A little bit of encouragement goes a long way. Teachers need encouragement, too! Write a note, send an email, or leave a message on email. We can live on a couple of words of praise for months.

8. *Stay positive even when things seem to be going negative.* Students may go through certain phases in their educational journey. A rough patch in the classroom might mold your child into a better student in the end.

9. *Assume the best before the worst of your child's teachers.* This maxim is generally good in all relationships. A teacher's heart is in his classroom everyday. Teachers want things to be positive for each of their students. Sometimes things may not appear as they seem and that is the time for good teamwork and communication.

10. *Be forgiving.* If a teacher doesn't get something quite right, remember that she is a human too. Forgiveness is a wonderful attribute in all of life.

Back to the playing field

Let's go back to the football game and the enthusiasm of that playoff game. Visualize that football field. The players this time are the students. The game being played is the game of their educational experience. They have been given their positions and their "plays." There are spectators in the stands consisting of their family and friends loudly and enthusiastically cheering them on in the game. Their number one fan is their parents. Down on the playing field with the students are the coaches. The coaches are on the sidelines guiding, going over winning plays, correcting bad plays, and coming up with a new ones. The coaches remain constant in their passion to see a win, but even more so, they are passionate about students giving their best and leaving it all on the field. They challenge them to keep going and never ever give up! These coaches are called "teachers."

Chapter

4

Lend a helping hand

"A teacher helps you learn so you get a lot smarter."
~Kindergarten student

I asked my kindergarten students:
"What do you think teachers do when all of the students go home?"
Here were some of their responses:
"The buses come back and take the teachers to go home, too."
"Clean the mess we made."
"They wait for their mommies and daddies to come pick them up."
"They stand in a line and wait to go home."

I have always wondered what students thought teachers do outside of school. Often it seems that they believe we live at school. I know this merely by the shocked faces that the students get after seeing me, their teacher, outside of school. "Mrs. Andrews, what are *you* doing here?" Which comes across to me as, "Mrs. Andrews, what are *you* doing outside the four walls of school?" This questioning is probably because I teach elementary school students; I am almost positive my mom does not face the same situation with her seniors in high school (that is, unless they're doing something they shouldn't be outside of school)! Fortunately, the parents of our students know that teachers are real people and have families and hobbies outside of school. So, it surprised me that after surveying hundreds of teachers across the country, the most repeated advice they wanted parents to know was how much time teachers spend working outside of school and how much they need parents' help. A lot of a teacher's time is taken making copies, cutting out projects, filing, entering student data, and filling out county paper-work. While all those tasks are important to the learning environment, if they were alleviated then more focus could be placed on lesson plans and creating a positive environment for the students.

For example, right now it is a beautiful, fall Saturday in my hometown in Georgia. The wind is light, the humidity low, and there is just a touch of coolness in the air. After the many blistering hot summer days, this mild weather is much appreciated by all who were able to step outside today. While most Georgians are spending a day like today on their lawns, on a picnic, or at the lake I, on the other hand, donned workout shorts, a college t-shirt, and pulled my hair back into a bun and am hovering over our recycling bin in the garage. Strange as it may seem, this has come to be a normal occurrence since I became a teacher. Whether it is the recycling bin, the trash can, or a closet, I spend many a Saturday searching for materials to use in the classroom for the follow-ing week.

Today I am on a quest for 16 plastic water bottles out of which my kindergarten students will perform a tornado experiment during centers. I have a bag of a few bottles that parents so graciously sent in, but I still need more. I know I am not alone in this act of after hour searching for "treasures." What many parents may not realize is that teachers are constantly thinking, looking, and planning for their classroom.

An elementary school art teacher shares, "I am constantly plan-ning for future lessons. Many days the last thought I have and the first thought I have are of ideas for art projects. When I read books to my kids at night I am developing new ideas for lessons. As teachers we are constantly working." Whether at the grocery store, the bookstore, or watching TV, most teachers' brains are still creating lessons and activities for their students. As one teacher states, "teaching is a job that requires just as much time, work, and planning outside of school as it does inside of school. As a classroom teacher there is always something that needs to be done. Our tasks are endless!"

Before my first year of teaching my mother forewarned me that teachers are teachers on and off campus in every way. Good teachers invest time-endless hours-creating. I feel blessed that I *expected* to put in countless hours outside the classroom, although most are not so lucky. Unfortunately, many teachers enter the field unaware of the time demands.

About half of new teachers leave the profession within the first 5 years, and one of the most common reasons for quitting is excessive workloads. It has not always been like this, but with the increase of laws, regulations, and parental expectations, the responsibilities tend to increase as well. I truly believe that no matter how much the undergraduate program may try to prepare future teachers, there cannot be enough preparation for what is about to come in the field of education.

So, what can parents do to help? There are hundreds of actions that parents can do to help teachers but we decided to keep it concise and find three of the most common pressures in teachers' lives; we then listed the most affective actions parents can do to help alleviate that pressure. We believe with a few more helping hands in each classroom, teachers can focus on providing more interactive and meaningful lessons for our nation's students.

A teacher's top 3 pressures:

1. Standardized tests

2. Buying materials for the classroom

3. Too little time to do too many things.

1. The truth about standardized testing

In recent years, a specific epidemic in education has increasingly become a stressor for teachers: *standardized testing.* In 2001, when the No Child Left Behind act passed, it required a means of knowing how schools were performing. As a result, standardized tests came about to measure the performance of neighboring schools. In theory this process sounds impressive. Even as an educator I thought it would be interesting to see how my school compared to others. But instead of a test that assesses the critical thinking skills of students, the standardized tests turned out to be tests of *how to take tests*. Do you remember the SAT, ACT or even the Boards Exam? All of those tests required previous practice of how to take the test. In order to be successful one had to learn the tricks, strategies, and skills of that test. The same is true for the standardized tests that we give our nation's youth. Teaching the material is not enough-not even if you teach it with experiments, discussions, or technology. Those strategies help but teachers still have to prepare their students for how to take the test since there is nothing else like it-sitting for hours, not talking, just listening, reading and bubbling in answers. I think my students are better than that, and they deserve better than that. Recognizing a correct answer out of a predetermined list of responses is essentially different from anything that people do in the real world.

Luckily US Secretary of Education, Arne Duncan, also believes that we need a change to our standardized tests. I was blessed enough to participate in the CNN filming of "Fixing America's Schools" with Arne Duncan and heard him speak about "dummied-down standards" of bubbling in answers, and how standardized tests need to focus more on critical thinking skills.[1] Hopefully we will see change in the future of standardized tests but for now the strict procedures of the test *alone* are enough to cause stress on anyone involved. Stress is such a small word but it has a huge impact. Over time the stress is a great distracter from our purpose as teachers, which is to enhance the knowledge of our students. I would love to see our schools go back to assessing the old fashion way with just final exams, chapter tests, and quarterly exams. It would save a lot of money, and it would alleviate the standardized test stress.

So why is standardized testing such a stressor to educators and students alike? Well, let's step into a teacher's shoes and see what it is like to teach with standardized tests…

•*Months before test week, teachers spend hours out of the normal school day just to practice test questions.* This reality means putting aside the science experiments, author studies, and technology projects in order to teach the students tricks to multiple-choice questions so they learn how to take the test.

•*Teachers must take the time to clear the room of any information that could be "helpful" for the students.* This "exam cleaning" means that everything the teacher worked so hard to put up to make the classroom comfortable must be taken down - only to be put back up later.

•*Teachers must attend numerous meetings to learn "proper test giving procedures."* Meetings occur in the late afternoon and attendance causes teachers to get behind on grades, lessons plans, and paperwork. In fact, I just spent an afternoon at one of these meetings and kindergarten does not even participate in standardized testing!

•*While giving the test, teachers must spend all morning reading from a script, and only from a script, as we watch the students struggle.* If we venture off of the script our jobs could be at risk in case something we say could be considered "cheating."

•*Teachers have to say "no" when a tearful student asks for help.* If teachers try to comfort a child or encourage one of our more reluctant students, we have violated the policy and our job may be at risk.

•*Teachers hope that no student has to use the bathroom during the test* or else the administration must be alerted and they have to notify the testing officials, so we could show we followed "proper test-giving strategies."

•*Teachers see the administration walking back and forth in front of the room* dozens of times to make sure we are not going off of the script and that we are following the rules.

•*After the test, teachers try to continue the curriculum*, which is fairly ineffective because the worn out students are unable to do anything because their brains are fried for the day.

•*Teachers also are exhausted at the end of tests days because we are frustrated from being test police.* Our feet are tired, we are dizzy from walking in circles around the students to make sure everyone is following procedure, and we are sick of our own voice; it is all we have heard the whole day!

•*Teachers have to deliver the good and often bad news about the tests results* and then console students who do not pass the test and their parents.

What parents see firsthand is the stress that standardized tests put on the children. From the outside looking in it appears that the teacher is to blame for creating and sustaining that stress, which is why one of the best ways you can help your child's teacher during standardized testing is simple-*understand*. That's it. Understand that we are following rules, not purposefully pressuring our students. I know firsthand how difficult it is to find a balance between teaching how to take a standardized test and teaching interactive and interesting lessons. There is only so much creativity that goes along with teaching the tricks of a multiple-choice test. The months prior to and especially during the test are stressful for both the teacher and students. Just understand that at times teachers might be overwhelmed and what they might need is a little grace.

2. Donations accepted here!

One strength that most teachers have in common is creativity. Teachers are pros at taking someone else's trash and turning it into a meaningful and fun lesson for students. I believe that it is a skill learned over time because even if a teacher does not start out a creative person, she eventually evolves into one after figuring out that salary and school budget do not allow for much more than the basic classroom essentials. That is why teachers love getting classroom donations. I don't care whether the item is new or used as long as I can use it for an activity. I remember reading an e-mail from a teacher that said, "You know you're a teacher if you get excited after a parent sends in bag of empty toilet paper tubes" (you'd be surprised what I can make out of an empty toilet paper tube).

"Teachers are pros at taking someone else's trash and turning it into a meaningful and fun lesson for students."

Ask your child's teacher if she has a "wish list" of items that are needed in the classroom. Do not feel obligated to send in all of the items; just send what you can. Teachers usually don't care if it is new or used; sometimes you just need to search around the house for something you no longer need but that creative teacher could put to good use. For example, just yesterday one of my students brought in a pile of books that she was finished reading, and I was more than willing to add them to my classroom library.

As much as teachers love to help families clean out their closets, we are not the only ones in need in the classroom. With our recent economy, many families are struggling, and educators are very aware of the difficulties that our students face. As one teacher says, "I teach in a school that is 90% on Free and Reduced lunch. The meals at school are the only meals these students receive all day. I often see students take extra just so they can bring it home to their mom, dad, or smaller sibling. It breaks my heart to see my students come in hungry. I usually bring in extra food knowing that I will give it away by the end of the day." I have met several teachers who save their children's old coats and sweaters to give to students in the winter.

Even more teachers shop at garage sales in order to buy books, toys, and clothes, if they know a family is in need. A fifth grade teacher discussed how one of her students came in everyday exhausted. It was not long before the teacher realized that since the parents were working 2-3 jobs, and the fifth grade student was left to make dinner for and take care of his younger siblings. This child had to live double roles, one as a ten-year-old student and the other as a homemaker!

The teachers who work at schools with students like these see firsthand what the children are going through. It is very hard to see such circumstances without stopping to help, which is why a lot of time is spent outside of school tutoring, counseling, and even attending events in order to support a student in need.

If your family is able to help, ask your child's teacher where there is a need in the classroom. Without disclosing a name, the teacher will be able to tell you what is needed-anything from winter coats and extra snack, to flashcards and books. Oftentimes it just means taking an afternoon of cleaning out your children's old clothes or books to bring in for a peer in need. You could also organize a neighborhood garage sale and donate the proceeds to the classroom teachers for supplied. Ask some neighbors, small groups, Sunday school groups to "adopt" a classroom family and meet their needs throughout the year. Any help is much appreciated by the teacher and especially by the student in need!

3. Racing the clock

In a typical workday, every minute a teacher has is already ac-counted for so, it is imperative that parents respect the teacher's time. If you need to talk to the teacher, send in a note with your child. The teacher can choose a time that she is available to meet. Please do not show up at the classroom door unannounced for a conference. I cannot begin to count the number of times parents, and even some teachers, interrupted my teaching in order to "talk" about an issue. The students' attention immediately turned to the other adult and my lesson quickly became useless. Even if the students are not in the room and a parent comes in to conference, it still poses as an issue. The "planning period" is usually a teacher's only time to do things like use the restroom, eat lunch, prepare for the next day, e-mail parents, or even just sit! So, think about what interrupting that time might mean for the teacher the rest of the day.

During my first year of teaching I had a mother enter my room to kindly talk about an issue in the classroom. She was very sweet, and actually had some wonderful points, but her unannounced meeting meant that I did not get to eat lunch that day. Unfortunately, it made it very difficult to be energetic the remainder of the school day. I am in no way saying to stay away from our classrooms. Of course, teachers want to communicate with parents.

"Any little bit of relief is much appreciated by teachers so they can focus on what's most important- your child."

We just like to know about it ahead of time. Send a note or an e-mail in order to give us a heads up, and at least we can prepare.

As you can see, a parent's help can take many different forms from calling ahead to announcing you're coming to sending in a box of crayons. Any little bit of relief is much appreciated by teachers so they can focus on what's most important: your child. There are three last ways you can lend a hand in your child's classroom and it all depends on the time you have available.

Hands-on help

If time is available and you would like to do something more tactical, you can work in the classroom. At our school a lot of teachers have "Monday Moms & Dads" who come in to help with whatever the teacher needs. Usually teachers have a desk outside their room, and on the desk they place the work with a note on top of what to do. During my first year of teaching I remember being absolutely amazed as I stumbled upon a hallway full of parents helping. I wonder if those parents knew what a great thing they were doing. Their assistance meant the teacher could put a little more focus on being present with the students.

I love when parents come to help in my classroom. Having an extra set of hands and eyes means that I can do activities that are challenging for the students yet require extra attention. As hard as I try, often when I do those challenging activities without another set of hands, it leaves the students frustrated and me worn out! As a parent you can even offer to work with a small group of students. Even if your child is not in the group, he/she is still being helped indirectly because while you are helping that small group it enables the teacher to ask questions or teach lessons that are more challenging to the rest of the class. More importantly those students are getting one-on-one attention that is often difficult to provide in a typical classroom setting. I know their parents would be very appreciative of your time!

Help from the home front

Time, however, is a rare commodity and not all parents have a couple hours to spend at their child's school tearing out papers from notebooks. If that is the case for you, there is another equally great way to help. If you want to help but cannot come in to school, offer to help from home. The teacher can just send home a project, like cutting or organizing, and you can do it all from your couch! Help is help whether you do it at home or at your child's school.

If time is just not an option for you, there is still another way to lend a hand. It may not seem like much, but just ensuring that your child's homework is completed and that any forms that are needed are turned in helps your child's teacher immensely. Juggling paperwork for 30-100 students is already overwhelming, and then on top of that comes deadlines to turn it in from the administration. Consequently, it is a huge relief to your child's teacher when parents return forms in an efficient and in a timely manner.

Look before you ask

Schools seem to constantly have an event to attend from Field Day to end-of-the-year celebrations. For parents it's hard to keep track of which one is which, when to be where, and what time to be where. *Teachers understand.* We are also keeping up with these dates but on top of that we are organizing the events and keeping up with our own children's events! So, how can you keep track of the events, while respecting the time of your child's teacher? Here are three helpful tips...

1. When you receive an invitation to a school event record it on your calendar right away! If you're too busy to do it, have one of your children be your "date keeper" and record all of your upcoming events to a calendar on your fridge. It is a great life skill for them to learn, and it helps you out. The school year can be very stressful, so encourage your family to work as a team to keep things organized. We do it in the classroom with "Classroom Jobs," and the students love taking ownership of the tasks.

2. When a teacher tells you a time of an event, do your best to arrive at that time. Every minute is accounted for in the classroom (for example my lunchtime is at *10:48*); so when an event is scheduled, most likely the teacher is working up to that time. For example I had a Mother's Day Tea in my classroom scheduled for 12:30. I am proud to say that all of the moms waited up in the front office and *then* walked down to my classroom at 12:30. It was such a huge help to me since right before the tea we were coming in from recess, having a bathroom break, *and* setting up. It allowed us to finish our classroom tasks, and the moms got to chat!

3. You know the old saying "look before you leap?" When it comes to your child's school events look before you ask. Most teachers include the date and time of events on their website, in their newsletter or on the invitation; so, before e-mailing or calling your child's teacher to ask the time and date of an event look at one of these places *first*. I know it seems quicker to just ask the teacher but remember that it is not just you asking. Most likely about half of the other parents are asking the same questions, which adds up!

In all honesty any little thing you can do to help ends up being a big help. You will rarely find a teacher who turns down a willing parent. As you can see, your time as a parent can drastically help your child's classroom environment. So, the next time an afternoon opens up, think about where your time would be most beneficial and perhaps shoot an email to an overwhelmed teacher offering to tear pages out of workbooks or organize the art drawer. Whether you come in to the classroom or help from your home, help is help and teachers appreciate *any* helping hand!

1.Duncan, Arne. "Fixing America's Schools." CNN. April 18, 2010. Television.

Chapter

5

Manners do matter

"A teacher is a person who teaches but also who helps us as students to make the right choices as we go through school and regular life experiences."

~High school student

Since I spend my time with the "big kids" all day I love to hear stories about Tiffany's sweet, little kindergarteners. Sometimes we share similar stories (despite the age difference) but most of the time she tells me the cutest stories that reflect only the innocence of a 5-year-old. One such story was about a particular little boy who Tiffany called, "the little gentleman." He earned his title because from day one of school he was the perfect little gentleman to Tiffany. He would say, "Yes ma'am" and "No ma'am," he would hold the door for her, and offer to carry her bags if she had her hands full. Of course, as her mother, my immediate thought was he must have developed a little crush. But Tiffany insists that he was like that to all of the students. In her words he had "wonderful manners." Eventually Tiffany asked the mother what she and her husband did to teach their son such amazing manners. The mother was very flattered but replied that she could not think of an exact answer. This is when Tiffany came to me and said, "How can they not know? I'm sure that he isn't learning those manners on TV." As a mother I knew that he was a living example to what was happening at home. Children are wonderful imitators of their environments. This little boy was most likely in an environment where manners were expected and practiced. Through example that mother was teaching her son wonderful skills that he will use his whole life.

Manners are a form of communication

Think of the last time someone showed you manners like opening the door for you, letting you cut in line because of your few items, or helping you carry a load of boxes. Without saying a word, what did that person communicate to you? Did you feel respected, honored, and valued? Now think of a time someone showed you a lack of manners. What did that person communicate to you? Did you feel disrespected or embarrassed? Manners, or lack of manners, are verbal or nonverbal ways to communicate to another human being. One of our goals as educators is to help students use their manners to become effective communicators. Students will use this skill for the rest of their lives with relationships, school, and careers. The school environment is filled with communication between students, teachers, parents, and administrators. From kindergarten through high school students are given numerous opportunities to learn how to communicate effectively.

The most successful communicators are those who display manners and treat others with respect. How one speaks to another person sets the tone in a positive or negative direction when communicating. Communication skills are needed more than ever in our world, and that includes our schools. Unfortunately this growth of miscommunication has caused many of the lawsuits that are becoming so prevalent in schools. There are obviously many things that cause a conversation or situation between two people to go negative. It takes a deliberate decision to be kind and do the best to converse positively with another person.

My classroom is a place where being polite to each other is expected. I want each of my students to be treated with honor from their peers and from me. However, on the rare occasion that they have a "differing moment," we have a solution to help students make the needed adjustments in their interaction with each other. We stop what we are doing and I say, "Class, what are the three ways to treat a person?" A burly football player , with his deep resounding voice leads his class and says, "Number one!" The class answers: "Be kind!" "Number Two!" The class answers: "Be kind!" "Number three!" The class gives the final answer: "Be kind!" They are quick to get the message and we continue our lesson for the day. I like to instill this little saying in their minds because I believe it to be true. One of the main things that help the students to be kind is to "put on" their manners.

> "The problem of bullying is being partially blamed on a lack of manners and respect on the part of the bullying student."

Putting on our manners

Putting on manners each day is making a definite decision to think of others and to be a considerate human being. Manners really do shape the way we react to others. Being polite and kind sends the non-verbal message to others that the individual desires to get along with people and show them respect. It goes without saying that it is much more pleasant to be around people with manners than those without. In the world of education it is becoming a concern that the lack of manners is causing other serious issues in our schools. It is being linked to students' overall behavior. The problem of bullying is being partially blamed on a lack of manners and respect on the part of the bullying student. Something must be done about the escalating number of bullying reports; this issue must be addressed without delay.

Manners are generally thought to refer to table etiquette but they involve much more than all the proper things to do when one is eating. In the southern part of the United States where I live, parents enroll their middle school aged children in "Cotillion." The purpose of these series of classes is to teach children proper etiquette. At a young age, the children are taught everything from the art of fine dining to ballroom dance. I have talked about Cotillion class with my high school students. It never ceases to amaze me how much they retain from the experience years before.

I remember the time a senior boy stood up and began doing the fox-trot in class to prove that he still remembered the steps! I applaud the parents who enroll their child in such activities even if they are met with resistance. The course is a wonderful tool for parents to use to help them teach their children social etiquette. Parents teach their children manners. By modeling good habits themselves, they are putting the non-verbal stamp of approval on a behavior or habit. Parents set the course of their child's life by small habits-good or bad.

Good home training

Individuals trained in good manners present themselves in a positive light. People often react to each others based on the way they were first treated. Like Tiffany's "little gentleman," good home training is the key to developing manners and respect in children. Manners vary from household to household because the parenting styles, cultural differences, and belief systems will all affect the specific manners being taught. Even though we live in a diverse and ever-changing world there are basic manners that span the course of time and are important for a child to learn. Remember the Golden Rule: "Do unto others as you would have them do unto you." Just imagine how much nicer things would be in the world if people would remember their manners.

Think about the way children are allowed to talk to adults. Consider their tone of voice, the words they use, and the manner in which they speak. I must admit, I have been surprised at the way I have observed parents talking with their children and vice versa. It is critical to set the tone in the home to speak in a respectful manner to one another. When these things are required at home, the child develops a habit of being mannerly when he enters school. It becomes a natural way of operating for the child. A child who speaks respectfully to a parent will speak respectfully to teachers.

Our culture has lost the focus of teaching manners. Perhaps it is seen as a stuffy or an outdated way to act. Parents have many demands placed on them and daily face busy schedules. Yet there are times in which we can instill or encourage manners. Cultural events (weddings, parties, celebrations) are a perfect time to teach children manners about how to interact with adults and handle formal social situations. Family dinners can offer a teachable moment. However, a leisurely dinner in the evening is often cut short due to a scheduled soccer practice, a creditor calling, or a crying baby. Many families are not eating meals together where the opportunity to practice table manners would be perfect. Social occasions have become more casual and informal. Despite all these challenges to the average American household, parents must find time and creative ways to train their children in the area of manners. Children will need manners in life. The business world hires people who exhibit social graces and good manners; often those skills were the result of home training.

Manners in the working world

Whether you are a job applicant or a company bidding for a job your skills can get you in the door but your people skills are what can get the job. The manners taught to your child help form her overall people skills. If your children have developed positive ways to interact with others, it will serve them well as they move into the work force. A confident young person is one who knows how to handle herself well in a variety of social settings. Good manners often give the student the foundation for success later in life. Punctuality is one of the first manners a future boss will observe. Parents can develop the habit of being on time with their child. The child who is always the last one to be picked up or whose parent has never been on time to a parent-teacher conference may pick up some habits that hinder her as she attempts to function in the business world.

Business owners have their own creative ways to evaluate prospective employees. I know several company CEO's who take prospective employees out to eat and out on the road to drive. When I asked why, they said that they can tell a lot about a person by the way he drives and how he handles herself in a restaurant. The prospective employee who shovels in food with both elbows on the table may be sending a negative message to the boss across the table.

Students will be heading out into the world to pursue their careers some day. Parents long for their children to get that dream job. Equipping and demanding that the child exhibit good manners will help her achieve success in the job search. One of my closest friends smiled as she told me how her son thanked her for teaching him manners. He told her it helped him to be chosen as a pilot for one the nation's largest airlines. Manners do matter.

Practice starts in the classroom

Our classrooms thrive when students practice their manners. One elementary school teacher includes the following phrase as part of the student's daily routine: "I will listen, follow directions, and be kind to others." Knowing how to be kind to others by using manners leads to respecting other people. On the first day of school, it is a breath of fresh air when a student arrives in my classroom and already displays respectful and mannerly behavior. It makes it easier for him to adjust to the expectations of my classroom as well. I make it a point to compliment those students exhibiting good manners and showing respect to each other. I enjoy catching students practicing their manners because the classroom environment benefits when students are respectful.

"Our classrooms thrive when students practice their manners."

The instructional time will flow better and learning takes place in a more efficient manner than when a teacher must stop instructional time to deal with behavior issues. As I mentioned earlier, I occasionally must remind my students "let's put our manners on today." At the end of the semester one of my students was "forgetting" to be respectful in the classroom. I turned around to hear one of my other students say "Hey, put your manners on!" Of course I had to smile at the echo of my words.

It is my goal to have a message sent to all my students that they will be treated with honor and respect in my classroom. I deliberately set the bar high because I want to be part of helping them grasp the importance and benefits of learning those skills. When those dynamics are in place, the tone of the class is more positive, peaceful, and upbeat; learning becomes collegiate and a cooperative process.

Where is the respect?

Manners and respect work together hand in hand. Some experts believe that you cannot have one without the other. We are living in a culture that does not always promote respect. Drivers can list the times they have experienced poor manners by other drivers. Think of the last time you went out to eat and observed disrespectful behavior exhibited to the waitress or waiter. I just traveled out of the country; remembering your manners and respect in the airport can be a challenge for anyone. Too often people just want what they want and don't care to be nice about it. My niece illustrated that self-focus when she commented that when someone has been rude to her verbally or otherwise she wonders if that persons remembers that she has feelings, too.

Although it appears that respect is diminishing, we have a choice to make. Everyday in some way we are all faced with choosing to handle people with respect. We all want to be treated with respect and honor. Instilling the character trait of respect in a child is critical. Understanding that adults should be respected gives the students the key and habit of honoring those in authority over them. The adults need to be the first in setting the example of what that looks like. Children are constantly watching and taking notes when observing adults in their world. Parents take the leading role in this area. When speaking to and about the teacher, parents need to model some degree of respect.Parents know when they have used an inappropriate adjective because of their anger; their children hear the destructive word. The parents set the standard for respect in the classroom by the way they discuss the teacher at home. We, as teachers, are in the schools benefiting from the home training that has taken place by the parents. Then, we work at reinforcing what the parents have hopefully already taught the students. Parents who have the expectations of respect in their home are giving their child a sense of security and safety. Human nature responds positively to honor and respect.

Being respectful is putting others' interests ahead of our own sometimes. It is having a good attitude even when we don't understand or agree with something. It is respecting the differences in another person's look, culture, or food; accepting each other as valued members of the community and classroom helps to promote an environment in which all can learn.

Notice manners in life

We are often affected by the choice that others make to show respect. This summer I rode on a trolley with other tourists up the side of a mountain. As the guide narrated the tour, we saw beautiful flora and fauna and enjoyed the wildlife before us. At the end of the tour, the tour guide paused before opening the door. He said, "I just want to thank you for being the most respectful well-mannered trolley I have had today. I really appreciate it. It made it so much more pleasant for me to give you the tour." We were surprised and said "thank you." People notice when we are courteous and think of others before ourselves. Good manners demand that we show appreciation for those who do demonstrate that kind of concern. I couldn't help but say, "It's the good home training!" We all laughed. He went on to describe the rude tourists who often push and shove for the best seat, show impatience when a question is asked, or who act bored by the guide's speech. We were that fresh breath of air to the trolley guide.

I have been in many situations that I used as teachable moments with my girls as they were growing up. When we witnessed certain behaviors, good or bad, I would take the opportunity to discuss what happened. The girls were very interactive and had many good suggestions and comments. It is once again important for children to feel a part of making the decision to be the type of person who is polite. Have them be on the look out for good manners; make a game of it. When they see that you value respect and good manners, they will seek to become like you.

10 of the most commonly used manners in the classroom.

If you need a guide for where to start, here are 10 of the most commonly used manners in the classroom. Start with these and then move on to others that you find important. While you read these, think if they are also important in your home and workplace. As you will see, manners are used throughout all stages of life. Why not start practicing early?

1. Punctuality. Be on time when someone is counting on you to be somewhere.

2. Learn to say phrases like "please," "thank you," and "excuse me."

3. Address elders with titles like Mr., Mrs., or Ms.

4. Do not interrupt when someone is speaking.

5. Take care of objects that are not yours.

6. Write thank you notes after an act of kindness or present is given.

7. Answer adults with responses like "Yes," "Yes ma'am," or "Yes sir," instead of "Yeah."

8. Open the door for someone, especially if her hands are full.

9. Do not leave a mess at lunchtime.

10. Wait your turn.

The way we treat each other in the home will flow over into the schools and life. Often, the home is the place where we let our "real" selves out. Could you say "please" and "thank you" more with your children? Sometimes we get in the role of "drill sergeant" and forget our manners at home – the most important place of all. Attention must be given to training a child in the area of manners and respect to interact better with people in life. Role-playing with your child inside the home is a great way to "practice" good manners. Have a "manners" jar – when someone is especially well mannered, put a quarter in the jar. When it is full, celebrate by taking the family out for ice cream or a favorite treat! As we are respectful and use our good manners, we help to create harmony wherever we are. Many resources are available to aid parents in training their children in all areas of manners and respect. They are easy to use and categorized by subjects.

Take the effort and energy to create situations to teach your child manners. Create a respectful home environment where children can "catch" how to do it. If your child exhibits poor manners, examine your home environment. If something needs to change, resolve to do so. The manners you teach your child now will last him a lifetime. One day, he just may come back and thank you!

Chapter

6

A compliment goes a long way

"A teacher is someone who says, "What's going on here?'"
~Kindergarten student

I asked my kindergarten students:
"What is the nicest thing someone has said to you?"
Here were some of their responses:
"Your dress is really pretty."
"I want to be your friend."
"You can play with me."
"I'm proud of you"
"I love you very much."

We use an average of 30,000 words a day, and as a parent your child is hearing at least half of them; so why not make your words count for something? The power of a positive word is a strong one. It is hard to be negative after receiving a genuinely kind word. Even Mark Twain once said, "I can live for two months on a good compliment." Just a few uplifting words can help you make it through a rough day, land a big deal at work, or even accomplish a dream. Similarly, the words you choose to use with your child will influence the path he will take in life. As a parent you must *select* the words you speak to your child; don't just *say* what comes into your mind first.

Before we talk about the words that you say to encourage your child we have to start at the foundation-*you*. A person must first learn to speak positively about him/herself before speaking positively to others. It is difficult to motivate others in a positive way if you are consumed with doubts and negativity yourself.

"As a parent you must select the words you speak to your child, don't just say what comes into your mind first."

The words you speak to yourself are the most important words you say all day. Whether you have a "can do" attitude or a "can't do it" attitude, your child will emulate what he sees.

Since I am a teacher I am going to give you an assignment to do before reading on in this chapter. Stop, take a moment and get out a piece of paper and answer these questions to the best of your ability (feel free to write multiple answers for each response):

- *What part of your life are you most proud of?*
- *What are your talents?*
- *What makes you happy?*
- *What are your proudest accomplishments?*

At five years old, the students in my class have already mastered this skill. On more occasions than I can count, I have complimented a student for a well-performed task only to hear back, "I *know* Mrs. Andrews. I'm good at that." So channel your inner child and don't be afraid to say what's great about you. Now that you have written down your answers you can refer back to them on rough days or days that you need a little extra encouragement.

Catch yourself before any negative thoughts enter your head because they don't belong there! Once you start to focus more and more on the positives about yourself, the negatives will start to lose their voice. Over time you will find that every time you accomplish a task there is a sense of pride that you "did it" whether it's completing a workout class or landing a deal at work. The end result is that you will be ready and able to encourage others (like your precious children)!

Complimenting your child towards success.

While complimenting your child will help in the home environment, it will also (like most things) spill into the classroom setting as well. Just like the Home and School Cycle mentioned earlier, if students hear that they can do it at home, they are more likely to come into the classroom and do it! When a student enters my classroom door with a "can do" attitude, I can't help but be thankful. As a teacher I get to see firsthand the power of a positive attitude on students. Our students arrive at school with additional factors such as ADD, ADHD, and Dyslexia, so it doesn't hurt to have an optimistic outlook on life. Some children are born optimistic while others might need more training. Either way the practice starts at home.

Children of all ages need to know when they are doing something right before they are told how they are messing up. No matter what age your children are you can still catch them doing something right from sharing a crayon to parking the car in the garage. Below are a few tips of how to select your words rather than just say them.

When giving a compliment...
- *Make it sincere*: Instead of an empty compliment, ensure that your compliment is honest.
- *Make it specific*: When you are specific about what you are complimenting, the other person can understand and appreciate your words even more.
- *Make it thoughtful*: Instead of giving a compliment just to give one, take the time to think about what you are complimenting. It is better to receive fewer meaningful compliments than many shallow compliments.
- *Make it personal*: The best compliments are those that are special to your relationship with the other individual.

The relationship between a parent and a child is unique and near impossible to imitate. But like every relationship there are ups and downs and sometimes it needs some help. Compliments are a simple yet powerful relationship-building tool. It makes sense that compliments help relationships because by giving a compliment you are taking the time to focus entirely on another person. Eventually the more compliments you give, the easier it becomes to find the positive qualities in others rather than the negative.

Educators often use compliments as a strategy for classroom management. Instead of scolding the misbehaving student, the teacher compliments the students who are following directions. Consequently the good behavior is recognized and the poor behavior is redirected. The affirmative words help provide a positive classroom atmosphere rather than a negative one. I have also seen this strategy work in the home environment. The more attention spent on the positive behavior, the more likely it will be repeated. Additionally, the more attention spent on poor behavior the more likely it will be repeated.

During our study for the book many parents voiced that they did not feel their words were received fully by their children. You, too, may feel that the hard work you put in to creating a "positive home environment" is not recognized by your child (especially if he/she is a teenager). Well, I have good news for you! Your children value you, and they value your time together. If they didn't, we wouldn't have to write this book because the teachers could do all the work in the classroom. But we know that our students' value lies with their family. Teachers can help set a firm foundation for your child, but we are not near as influential as you, the parent.

A little praise can change a day

The affects of the words you choose to say don't just stop at your child; they can affect your child's teacher as well! When teachers are encouraged and uplifted by parents and/or students, it helps us work to the best of our ability. As you saw in previous chapters, a lot of work goes into each school day and for someone to notice and say something means the world to a teacher! Consequently, the words parents say to the teacher can help create a positive environment for their children.

Luckily, about 95% of the encounters between parents and teachers are positive. More and more parents understand the importance of this "other adult" in their child's life, and as a result, are communicating, helping, and supporting teachers. On the other hand, most teachers have had at least one confrontational occurrence with a parent during their career and vice versa. Whether it is a Teacher-of-the-Year, a first year teacher, or a veteran teacher, teachers have had their fair share of parents who are not pleased with them and let it be known to whomever is listening.

For example one day I experienced a challenging conversation with a parent that ended up not going as well as I had hoped. It made for a challenging morning but then something happened during lunch that changed my whole day. While I sat at my desk, another parent from my class came in with her daughter who was returning from a doctor's appointment. After helping her daughter unpack and sending her down to the lunchroom, the mom stayed around to talk with me. Her words were ones that I will always remember because the timing could not have been more perfect. She simply said, "You know, I just wanted to tell you that we are so happy that our daughter has you as her kindergarten teacher. You are doing a wonderful job caring for these children." That's it! Just two sentences, yet it changed my whole day. I am positive that the mom still does not know how helpful her few words had been, or that I cried when she left. But how could I explain it to her without gossiping about another parent? I couldn't. All I could say was, "Thank you. I really needed that." And I did.

Think back to the compliments you have given to your child's teacher. Did you ever think that they could have been just what the teacher needed in order to make it through the day? As teachers we are very limited to what we can divulge about other parents and situations with students (and rightfully so). Parents will never be able to know the whole story. What you can know is that whether the teacher is having a good day or a bad day, a compliment only makes things better.

I do not intend for parents to compliment each idea and effort from the teacher. But if something deserves a positive accolade feel open and welcome to say so! Just a quick e-mail or note in your child's folder does the trick. So often teachers feel like they blend in with the other accessories in the classroom - unnoticed but expected to be there. But if a mistake is made, we are suddenly noticed. As a nation we have inadvertently designed a system in which being good at what you do as a teacher is not acknowledged, while being poor at what you do is often scrutinized. Instead of waiting until something negative

"The compliment that you gave your child's teacher could have been just what the teacher needed to make it through the day."

happens to communicate with your child's teacher, use the opportunity of a positive situation to voice your opinion. If you give praise long before criticism, it will most often be taken as positive criticism rather than negative criticism.

I use the same strategy with my students' parents. Parents are more apt to listen to the concerns I have about their child if I have already made it known that I respect and love their child. They need to know their child's positive qualities before the introduction of any struggles their child has. Work first on establishing a foundation of respect free of judgment. Only then can the relationship be built and will others accept your critiques as valid.

Most of the time it will be easy to find something to compliment your child's teacher about, but at other times you might face teachers where it is not so simple. If you are starting to see the importance of encouragement but don't know where to start, look back at the list of simple strategies to use when giving a compliment. And if you are like me and need an example, below are some responses by teachers who thought back to their most memorable compliment. These were teachers inexperienced and experienced and from all over the country but all would agree that a compliment goes a long way.

I asked the teachers:

"What is the best compliment you have received from a parent?"

Here were some of their responses:

• "Not only were you a teacher to my child this school year, but you were his mother when I couldn't be with him during the school day."

• "Thank you for helping my child want to come to school each day."

• "You not only taught my child how to read, write, and do math, but you helped my child grown as a responsible citizen and American."

• "You have made this first experience as parents a relaxing year. More importantly [our daughter]'s impression of school has been incredibly well-rounded by your guidance and leadership. Your creativity, dedication, genuine concern, and passion for what you do shine through. You have an incredible natural talent and are truly gifted. I hope you always maintain your drive and passion so that countless more lives can be touched in the way you have with [our daughter]."

• "Mine came from a parent of a child who had (at the time) non-diagnosed Asperger's syndrome and was having a very hard time adjusting to his new school. He had hurt me physically (stabbed with a pencil, hit in the head with a book, desk thrown at me, chairs thrown at me, punched in the stomach and chest, etc.) many times during the year. When we (the school workers) decided something wasn't right, we talked with the mom about possibly testing him. We were all nervous about how she would react but instead of frustration and tears, she said "You are the only teacher he has ever had who has taken the time to get to know my child and know that he is not a devil, and that something is truly wrong – he's not just a bad kid! I am forever grateful!" Turns out he has severe Asperger's and now he is a VERY successful middle school student in the general educational setting! She also sent a letter to the superintendent! That made my year, and made me feel like I could accomplish ANYTHING!"

- "At the beginning of the school year I always start out telling my students about my Type 1 diabetes. I explain what it is, what I have to do in order to keep my body healthy, and what the students should do in case anything ever happens to me during the year. Soon after I talked to the students about my diabetes, we had Open House at our school. I was pleasantly surprised when one of my students' dads came in to thank me for talking about diabetes. He said his son had only been diagnosed with the disease a few months prior and their family was still getting used to the lifestyle. Hearing me speak about my own battle with diabetes had helped his son realize that one can have a normal life despite the disease. His words meant so much to me that I became tearful as I spent the next hour talking to him about tips, websites, and books that would help their family become accustomed to life with a diabetic. Even though it has nothing to do with my teaching, it meant so much to me that I had helped that family in some way."

Bring compliments into your professional world

Unfortunately, the giving and receiving of compliments is a basic need that does not get met often in our fast-paced, media-hyped, technical world. Too often individuals run through life much like one would run a race. We focus on the task ahead, or "finish line," while ignoring the people running alongside of us. If individuals could take a moment to turn to the right or left and say "Good job," now and then, we might all find it a little easier to get through the day. It turns out that the value of a compliment is not just true of teachers; any professional likes a good compliment now and again. You may be an optimistic loner in your office but your words could eventually help your workplace to be considered "a great workplace."

As I said before, life is full of cycles and if you have a positive workplace it helps you stay more positive about yourself. Consider the effect your words could have on one of the most powerful workplaces – the classroom. Even though you cannot be in the classroom daily, you can positively affect the environment where your son or daughter spends the day. Take the time to assess yourself; are you influencing your home and your child's classroom in a positive manner? If not, choose to do so. Even the most negative, pessimistic of characters, Uncle Scrooge, found a way to find the joy again. If you are a positive individual, it helps you be a positive influence to your child, which ultimately influences the environment of the classroom! Whew!

Chapter 7

Stand strong as a parent

"A teacher is a role model and teaches you about life."
~High school student

One of the most joyous events in life is the birth of a precious child. The minute the baby is born, the parents can barely grasp the miracle they are holding in their arms. They immediately are deciding who the baby looks like the most and whose eyes, nose and mouth the baby got. The love they feel is overwhelming and deep. I have often heard parents say that they never realized they could love something so much. This tiny little human being is full of potential and promise. The parents have dreams for their child before they even leave the hospital. It is a wonderful and happy occasion.

I remember coming home with my first daughter. I was laying her in her crib and suddenly had this feeling of panic and thought, "*Now what do I do*?" The profound responsibility of taking care of this beautiful little girl hit me at that moment. Parents feel that sense of responsibility and desire to do the right thing for their child. We read books, go to doctors, and talk to seasoned parents all in our effort to be diligent parents. Parents become protectors and educators of this tiny new person. If you are a parent you know that parenting is not for cowards. It is a life long journey of love and devotion.

79

As parents, we want to do all we can to set our children's lives in a direction that will help them to be all that they can be. We want to guide them in developing good habits in their lives. Even from the time they are tiny, we can begin to instill those habits by practicing them on a daily basis. But instilling good habits in another human being is not an easy task! This chapter is not called "Stand *by* as a parent," it is called "Stand *strong* as a parent;" meaning the task ahead might get tough at times but your efforts will be rewarded! By following the tips in this chapter you will create an environment for your child that will enable him to respect you, honor you, and feel secure in the fact that he has a strong authority figure looking out for him.

Set a routine

When my girls were very young, one of the first tips my pediatrician suggested was that I develop a routine each day. He stated that children do better and function best when they are on a schedule. They sleep better, eat better, and are less fussy. I agree because I saw it work with my daughters. Routine and schedule are often difficult to put into place due to our busy lives. There are just "those" days sometime, which is understandable. It is wise to do all that is possible to establish a sense of order in the children's day by setting their routine. It is a first step in developing those good habits in the life of the child for now and in their future.

In earlier chapters we have talked about the parent being the first teacher. Parents instruct their children every day of their life. On occasion, the routine must change and needs to be flexible. With family functions, social events, and as working parents, you might have to falter from the routine and that's okay. After you do get off schedule, just try to get back to the routine as soon as you can. Children thrive on a schedule of order and routine on a regular basis. It is predictable and it helps children to know what is expected of them as they grow up. Parents and homes have different personalities ranging from easy going to more structured. Since parenting styles vary, every family's "routine" will look different. Parents will have to figure out by trial and error what works best for their family.

As children grow up, they continue to function best with structure and routine. Having predictable patterns of routine in the life of a child makes life flow better. I have observed the routine that Tiffany has in her kindergarten classroom. She has certain daily routines that are consistent each day. She tells me that when these routines are disrupted she spends the rest of the day trying to recover from it. When the children get out of their routine they have a hard time settling back in to the instructional time. It makes handling the children more difficult for the teacher or parent when this happens. It is no different on the high school level. When we

"Having predictable patterns of routine in the life of a child makes life flow better."

have assemblies, fire drills, and events at school, it takes some time getting the teens back on track and focused on learning.

When Tiffany finds that her classroom routine is changed, a strategy that she has used and found successful is to write the day's events on the board in order. She prepares the class for the change, explains the day's order, and then the students get to check off the events as they occur. It is a visual reminder as to what the day will hold since it is something new. This is a strategy that parents can easily do at home. Write down the day's events on a piece of paper and post it on the fridge. Have the children take turns checking off the events as they occur. We do it in our adult lives with "to do lists" so why not start learning the strategy early on?

Create structure

I have observed over time that my high school students function best with structure versus unstructured lessons. They like to know what is expected of them. I noticed that when the guidelines are too loose they tend to get distracted and off task. Students like and need guidelines to accomplish an assignment. At first I might get resistance but once I remind them that this is the "game plan," they do (reluctantly) comply, and eventually it becomes a habit. A basketball coach would never tell his team to go out on the floor and just figure out what to do. He gives his team a definite strategy to play the game. Teachers of any age level will agree that more learning takes place when there is a strategy in place in the classroom. Sometimes the lesson calls for what I like to call "unstructured order." The students are involved in an active lesson that appears unstructured. However, behind it is a purpose for the lesson and a certain result to be achieved.

Routine and structure are very similar, and often run hand in hand. The difference is the routine you set are the tasks and patterns you accomplish *daily* while structure is the organization that you bring to your *lifestyle*. Parents create structure in their homes in a variety of ways. In some homes structure may look like:

- Having a set dinnertime or bedtime.
- Establishing daily/weekly chores for each child.
- Cleaning out the playroom once a month.
- Keeping a calendar posted with the family's activities.
- Posting family rules in a common room.
- Maintaining a bedtime routine such as a bath or story time.
- Having set consequences for certain bad behavior.

No matter what your "structure" looks like, students who have learned the importance of organization and structure at home handle it better in school. It is expected of them at school and also later in life in the workplace. Students feel better about themselves when they accomplish what is expected of them. I have seen students who seem to wander through their school experience. They can't locate their papers, they leave assignments at home, forget to do the assignment at all, and don't seem to have a plan to get it done. They get down on themselves or else hide it by being indifferent. Unfortunately they are developing negative habits in their lives. Even the most unstructured personalities can learn tools that will help them function in situations that require a routine or structure. At any age, students who develop the quality of self-discipline and structure set themselves up to achieve success in their life. Parents are the key to setting the expectations for their child to bring this about, by setting boundaries and guidelines for children.

Parents and boundaries in the home

Students of all ages need parents who are not afraid to set boundaries and guidelines for them. There will come a time when the children will challenge the parent's expectations. Parents must stand their ground when setting rules for their child. You are the parent and know what is best for your child. Parents are the authority in the life of their child. Being a good leader means sometimes making unpopular decisions for the good of the children. It is not fun to withstand some of the reactions that come from such a stand. Nonetheless parents need to do what they feel is best and stand strong. It is such a temptation to give in to keep everyone happy but be determined and focused on the end result- a child who respects, honors you and feels secure in knowing that they have a strong (not weak) authority figure watching out for them.

"Students of all ages need parents who are not afraid to set boundaries and guidelines for them."

Parents need to be parents not friends to their children. The friendship phase will come into your life later on when they are grown adults. Expectations and guidelines may not always be received well, but they need to be put into place. Parents need a game plan when it comes to guiding their child through his schooling as well as life. It is beneficial to write expectations and family guidelines down and post them on the refrigerator or other prominent place in the house, so the children can read them on their own and the parents do not have to repeat themselves. Teachers post their rules in the classroom as well so it will be a familiar strategy for your child. Older children can be included in the decision making process of goals and guidelines. Including the children gives them a sense of ownership in the decisions and they will be more likely to follow them. Family meetings are also an effective way to communicate expectations with children. Parents can express at that time their thinking and their heart for the child.

Prioritize your activities

I encourage parents to place a high value on academics, which seems easier when the children are young. Younger students get excited to get homework. By the time I get them in high school, they have many distractions that pull them away from their job as a student, and they don't have time for homework. I tell my students: "Do your have-to's first and your want-to's last." It helps to place a priority on ordering our "to do" lists. I "want" to go shopping today, but I "must" pack for a trip I am leaving on tomorrow.

I use this saying with my students all year to help them realize how they are prioritizing their schoolwork and lives. If their parents demonstrated how to prioritize when they were younger, prioritizing becomes an easier and more natural task as they get older. Parents of younger children are much more involved in the overseeing of their children's to do lists and schoolwork. As the child moves up into middle and high school, the reins are gradually being handed over to the student. It is so important to insist that academics are finished before participating in other activities. My high school has study sessions prior to sports practices. This habit reinforces the importance that the school places on the concept of academics first. It teaches the students a good work ethic and prepares them for college and their careers.

Parents can keep children accountable by staying involved and asking questions. I encourage this practice even in high school. Ask a freshman child if the biology is finished and occasionally ask to see the homework and the assignment. As they see you checking not only that it was done but also done with a sense of pride and with a goal of completing the assignment, they will begin to take more ownership and pride in their assignments. Parents should require finished homework before socializing or time on the computer. At all ages the parents need to let their child know that they will be in communication with their teachers. Students learn how to be selective about what they tell their parents in regards to their schoolwork. Many schools post lesson plans and assignments on line or provide a handout that the parent signs.

Parents can review what is happening in their child's class and monitor their child's work. If there are any questions, contact the teacher. If what what your child is telling you is giving you mixed signals about a class, contact the teacher and get firsthand information. I appreciate the parent who contacts me first before coming to a conclusion. Even the most wonderful students may conjure up a story that will keep them out of trouble. A wise parent will be aware that this may occur and check out all sides of the situation. When they need to, they can award consequences to help send the message to their children reminding them of their expectations and guidelines.

Design consequences that work for you

Parents design the consequences for their children, and they know what means the most to their children if they had it taken away. When it relates to schoolwork, it is time to make use of that consequence when the child does not follow through and hold up his end of the deal. Students will tell me that if they just complain and whine long enough, their parents will eventually give in to them. Stand strong parents and stick to your guidelines! I have been guilty of giving in because it just seems easier for that moment. What I have realized is that the child senses that she has control, and as a result, I lose some of her respect. Children will continue to demand more and more control if they feel they can get it. After all, they want things to go their way no matter what the situation. Sometimes it just cannot be their way. The parent must take action when infractions have taken place. It is also appropriate if parents decide to give warning to their child. Sometimes the child will get the message the best using that approach. The bottom line is that children need accountability.

Strategies for dealing with your child are endless. Each family needs to decide how they will approach dealing with a child who is not putting effort into his schoolwork. As mentioned earlier, being a parent sometimes means taking the role of the unpopular person. It will pay off in the end. It is important for your child to see who is in charge. The child will try and take over the reins many times. Their security comes from the fact that they know they are not in charge, but they have parents who are in charge. Remember that a strong parent produces a secure child. Lots of love and perseverance on the part of the parent will help through the tougher times with their child.

To help you in standing strong, I have highlighted ten tips that will help parents stand strong as they guide their children through their years in school.

10 Tools to Help Parents Stand Strong

1. Establish a structured routine in your home starting in infancy. Developing a daily routine will help your children use their time wisely and develop good habits of discipline as they grow up.

2. Incorporate schoolwork in the daily schedule. For example, after a child arrives home from school have a plan. Perhaps the first 30 minutes will be spent eating a snack, playing with the dog outside, or reviewing information sent home from school. Then, schoolwork is completed before the next activity. The parent determines the time frame.

3. Take the first minutes to hear about your child's day. Allow your children to tell you about their day the minute you get them from the bus or pick them up. I have discovered that if I didn't capitalize on these first minutes I would lose the opportunity to hear about their day because they either lost interest or got distracted. If they have short or no answers that is ok, too. Just asking them about their day is what is important.

4. Decide on definite expectations you have for your child regarding their schoolwork. Every parent will need to decide on specifics of what they want to see accomplished with their children. I suggest setting aside time to think through their school schedule and write down your expectations and guidelines that you want to implement. Review them with your child and ask if they have any questions and discuss it with them.

5. Set precise goals for the class in which your child is enrolled. When they are enrolled in multiple classes, set goals for each class. I recommend that children are involved in this process, so that they feel a sense of ownership for the goals being set.

6. Check out information when there is a problem. Realize that students can be selective in what information they convey to their parents. It is a wise policy to contact the teacher if a problem arises.

7. Establish appropriate consequences. Your child should be aware of these consequences. They need to be consequences that will encourage the child to do what is right. If needed, stand by your consequences and carry them out. Do not give into pleading or promises that it "will never happen again." The consequence should ensure that your child will think before doing/not doing that action again.

8. Hold your children accountable for their schoolwork. Students need to take ownership of their schoolwork. Taking pride of their work is very important for their self-concept. As they grow older, the parent will gradually turn more of the reins over to children while still staying involved.

9. Be willing to stand strong for the good of your children even when they are not happy about it. Even when decisions are unpopular and individuals are upset, in the end well-formulated consequences are often what must be done to change behavior.

10. Find a great network of other parents with children the same age as yours. They are a wealth of information and ideas to aid you in guiding your children through their schooling. Building a network of supportive parents is often a lifeline for parents. They may have ideas you have not tried that will work better with your child.

I have two amazing daughters who light up my world. I am so proud of each of them. They are now grown and I am enjoying the friendship stage with my daughters. They were wonderful to raise and we had a lot of fun times when they were children. There were times that I had to stand strong and set guidelines for the best interest of my daughters. All parents face those times and issues. I think they would even agree that the parent must be the one in charge all the way along. The parents need to be large and in charge as they say. Your child's future depends on it. Every parent's style of standing strong will look different, as it should. Families are wonderfully diverse and unique. The one element that helps navigate through the times when you must stand strong as a parent and not a friend is love. Here's to the love we have for our children and their future and the devotion to help get them to a place of success.

Chapter

8

Practice T-R-U-S-T

"A teacher is somebody who teaches you things that you need to learn. They help you get to the right website if you need them to get you there."

~Kindergarten student

No matter what your job is, we all have to put our trust in something or someone everyday. When you get in your car to drive to work you are trusting that the car will run and get you to your job safely. At work you trust that your computer will function smoothly, save all of your important documents, and remain untouched by viruses. You even trust the chair beneath you to hold and maintain your weight. But the moment that trust is broken, it is very difficult to win it back. If your car breaks down, you might choose to shop for a different make and model entirely. If your computer fails you, you might trade it in for a different model or spend money on fancy programs that ensure it doesn't happen again.

While we all know a thing or two about trust, there is one demographic that knows more than most about trust and they are - parents. Once children enter the picture, parents must put their trust in everything from the food the child eats to whom the child is with. Once the child is school-aged, the parents must trust an individual with their little one everyday. Consequently teachers are given the gift of trust from parents each day. Many times this is as an easy task for parents, especially if your child has been blessed with trustworthy educators. But if your trust has been broken with a bad experience or you have seen too many horror stories on the news, then trust is hard to give. My hope for you is that after reading this chapter you will find that trusting your child's teacher, although not always easy to do, can be beneficial for your child's education and the classroom atmosphere.

When teachers know they have the trust of the parents it encourages them to maintain it on a day-to-day basis. Obviously a person does not become a teacher for the large paycheck, recognition, and glamour. Becoming a teacher is a choice; it is a passion. I can't count the number of times people have said, "I don't know how you do it," once they find out my profession. The funny thing is I wouldn't choose to do anything else! Of course it is not at all easy but it is rewarding. Even on the toughest of days, I come home knowing that in the long run I am making a difference.

Teachers also realize that we are the "other adults" in students' lives. That is not only a big honor but also a big responsibility! Recognizing the responsibility explains why parents' trust is so meaningful for a teacher. It's reassuring, encouraging, and it lets us know we're doing something right. Since trust is a difficult concept anyways, we decided to make an easy acronym that will help you take the needed steps to start trusting your child's teachers and showing it:

T: Take time to get to know your child's teacher.
R: Recognize, first, that your child's teacher is a professional.
U: Understand that the classroom is a very different and complex environment compared to home.
S: Select a focus.
T: The untold issues.

T-R-U-S-T

Take time to get to know your child's teacher.

Trusting someone you do not know is nearly impossible, so in order for you to trust your children's teachers, you must take the time to get to know them! Time is a rare commodity to come by these days, but when it comes to your child's education your time couldn't be put to better use. You may be asking, *is it really worth it?* My advice to you is to look back at the introduction. Your children spend 8 hours of everyday with their teacher. As a result, different rules, guidelines, mannerisms, and rituals are influencing your child every day. If you take the time to get an idea about the environment your child will be in and the person leading and creating that environment for the next year, then it will save many questions and concerns you have later on.

So how do you go about getting to know your child's teacher? Here are a few tips and events that you can attempt to make a priority in your schedule. Some of them take physical effort while others are as simple as clicking a few buttons!

• *Do your best to attend open school-wide events such as Open House, Curriculum Night, and Parent-Teacher conferences.* These events are meant to allow you to scope out the classroom. It is not a one-on-one meeting with the teacher, but it is your chance to see your child's daily environment. While there, ask yourself the following questions: How is the overall organization of the room? What behavior plans are in set? What are the classroom rules? By looking at the posters, books, etc. around the room, what is the teacher's focus What kind of technology is present? What kinds of materials are available? Are there any materials lacking that you could help supply (i.e. books, games, journals, craft items)? Sometimes you will have to ask the teacher in order to answer the questions if they are not apparent by just looking around the room. Just remember that the teacher might be overwhelmed with questions from the other parents as well; so make it short and sweet!

• *Read your child's syllabus, so you are aware of the teacher's focus, requirements, and policies.* Sometimes you might not even have to ask questions if you take the time to sit and read the packet the teacher hands you at the beginning of the year. The packets might appear daunting but they are filled with information about the teacher, the school, and the classroom. If you are already at the school for Open House, take the time to sit down and read through the material to answer any questions you might have. Then if you still have questions you are already there at school and can ask! You can even return to the syllabus if you have a question later in the year.

- *If available look at the teacher's website.* First of all, the website shows you how comfortable the teacher is with technology. Then you can look to see if there is an "All about me" page, a teacher philosophy page, or classroom news. All of these items will give you a better grasp of who this individual is who your child spends so much time with!

- *Volunteer in the classroom.* One of the best uses of your time is to volunteer in your child's classroom. Whether your children are in elementary, middle, or high school, their teacher could always use a helping hand. As a volunteer you can see firsthand what your child's day entails as well as the teacher's teaching style.

T-**R**-U-S-T
Recognize, first, that your child's teacher is a professional.

When people experience unfamiliar symptoms in their body they usually turn to the doctor for help. People look to the doctor knowing that he or she will have the knowledge and skills to help. Once in the doctor's office it is easy to look around and see the tools that the doctor is trained to use for various cases. Most likely the unfamiliar symptoms that brought the person to the doctor's office in the first place aren't at all unfamiliar to the doctor. Oftentimes the doctor has already been trained for, worked on, or seen a similar case before. As a result, the doctor is the best practitioner for the ill person to acquire optimum health.

As a doctor is a professional in the field of health care, teachers are professionals in the field of education. Teachers have the knowledge, skills, and tools to educate students of all personalities and learning styles. Most likely a student's learning disability or behavior issue is not new to a teacher. Oftentimes the teacher has already been trained for, worked on, or seen a similar issue before. As a result, the teacher is the best practitioner for the student to acquire optimum education.

Although teachers do not attend school nearly as many years as a doctor, the increase in national teacher standards has encouraged university programs to make education programs even more difficult and competitive. Many educational programs have become 5-year programs in order for teachers to graduate with both a bachelor's and master's degree. There is also an increase in field experience for educational programs. Teachers-in-training spend about 2 years worth of in-class experience before even stepping foot into their own classroom. As one teacher stated, "We are professionals, having gone through years of education and preparation. Several teachers have multiple degrees. Our training is filled with in-the-classroom hands-on experiences. We are very qualified at what we do and capable of making decisions for our students."

The key to trusting your child's teachers is to see them for who they really are- *professionals*. Trust that the tools, skills, and knowledge that the teacher has will help your child succeed in school and in life. If there is a tough decision to be made about your child, have faith that the teacher has experienced a similar decision in the past. Trust that if the teacher is new to your situation, there are seasoned professionals next door, upstairs, and in the front office who will guide her to the best course of action. Hundreds to thousands of students have passed through their classroom doors, so the teacher is your best chance at making a wise choice for your child's future.

T-R-**U**-S-T

Understand that the classroom is a very different and complex environment compared to home.

While writing this book I had the privilege of talking to a woman who was not only a wonderful mother but was also a leader in her company. Like many working moms, this mother described how she has become used to being two distinct people between work and home. At work she described that she "displays little emotion, remains in power, and delegates." But as soon as her foot enters the door at home she "is "Mom" who is full of emotion, is gentle, and displays love and support to her husband and children." Although it is the same woman, she is in two completely different environments. Both environments have their own rules, routines, and expectations. As a result, the mom has developed certain strengths and habits according to the environments in which she is.

A child also has two different environments-school and home. What most parents don't realize is that these environments are very different from one another. As one teacher stated, "Parents look at their child in an isolated, at-home environment and often don't understand the complex cognitive, social, and behavioral issues that arise when placed into a group setting at school." When children are in the classroom setting, they face many more factors than they do at home. In many cases, these factors can affect a child's temperament, behavior, and personality. There are three major differences between the school environment and the home environment.

#1 Social factors

Upon entering the classroom, students are required to work alongside around 20 different students. That means 20 different backgrounds, personalities, learning styles, and habits, which is quite an adjustment compared to only having to work alongside brothers and sisters at home! To a student, the same room could be filled with someone they dislike, like, or are scared of. Also, many teachers these days are lessening the teacher-focused classroom of having a teacher lecture the entire class and instead are turning to student collaboration as a means to learn. As a result, students are required to work in partners and small groups to complete a project, paper, or presentation. This method of learning adds even more components to the already complex socialization of the classroom.

Students, no matter what age, just want to "fit in." Depending on the personalities, beliefs, and backgrounds of your child's peers this could affect your child to be more outgoing, shy, forward, inquisitive, comical, or it could affect her hardly at all. This isn't a bad thing either. We are the same person no matter what but the people, experiences, and environments that we surround ourselves in help us become who we are as adults. The school environment is part of your child's walk through life.

"The key to trusting your child's teacher is to see them for who they really are- professionals."

#2 Management.

Every year students enter a new classroom with a new teacher, new rules, and new expectations. Classroom environments come in all shapes and sizes. They can be laid back, strict, calm, chaotic, organized, eccentric, technology-based, text-based, teacher-centered, or student-centered. As a result, every year your child has to adjust to a new set of rules, rituals, and guidelines. Such a yearly change is very different from the home environment where your child has had the same rules, rituals, and guidelines since birth (with maybe a few minor adjustments). This yearly change can be easy for a child who adjusts well to change but for those who like consistency it can be challenging.

As adults we face similar shifts in rules through our jobs. One job position may require you to dress, act, speak, and manage a certain way while another might be the exact opposite. In life we learn to adjust and learning how to adapt helps to make us who we are. From the changes in environment we learn what we like, don't like, or would like to try.

On a side note, if your child is part of a divorced family, do your best to have similar rules in both households. When children have two sets of rules and guidelines at their parents' home, and they are changing rules every year at school, they tend to get confused. Often these children shut down or "space-out" to block the confusion. I see this especially in kindergarten because the students are young and already trying to learn what is right, wrong, and acceptable. No matter how different you are as parents, it is much easier on your child if you work to make the rules consistent, which means similar morning routines, bedtimes, punishments, and praises. Of course it can't be identical, but the more you work to make it consistent the easier it will be on your child, and the easier it will be on you in the long run.

#3 The requirements

Regardless if the classroom environment is laid-back or strict, the main requirements stay the same. Students are required to remain focused and participate in class throughout the day. Teachers desire that students work to their best ability no matter if the students are doing hands-on activities, listening, or discussing a topic. As a result, students need to come to school ready to work each day.

At home, though there may be some work time, it is often a much more relaxed environment. The student is in his own environment with his family, his room, and his toys. They can relax, be themselves, and just do what they do best. Even if your child doesn't seem to love "family time," what most children won't say is that home is where they feel *most* comfortable. Whether it is in their room, on the computer, in front of the TV, or playing outside, home is comfortable because it is what children are used to. Do your best to let them relax and just be a kid.

Of course I know there is studying, homework, and projects to do, so encourage your children to pace their time spent on schoolwork, so they also have time to relax. Spend short amounts daily on schoolwork rather than large amounts on single days. If this means cutting out an extra activity then do it. Of all people, parents should know that life gets busy fast. While your children are in elementary, middle, and high school, let them be young. Soon enough they will face the same day-to-day busyness you experience. Perhaps they will be a little less stressed once they enter adulthood if they have fewer hassles as children.

As you can see there are a lot of factors that could affect a child's "normal" behavior in the classroom. A usually loud child could be shy and quiet. A normally quiet child could be the class clown. A well-behaved child at home could be a troublemaker in the classroom (and vice versa)! The classroom setting affects students in many different ways good, bad, and minimally. The best course to take is to talk with your children about their classroom environment. If your child is not a talker, then become aware of her education yourself through volunteering, reading the syllabus, or looking at the classroom website.

I've had so many parents say after a conference, "Are we talking about the same child?" Yes, we are. It is the same child but it is that child in two completely different settings. It is so easy to ignore what the teacher says, if it is "not like" your child. Trust that the teacher just wants to help, listen to what he sees in the classroom, and use it to further understand your child. As one teacher states, "If I could pick one thing for parents to know that would help their child, it would be trust that the teacher has your child's best interests in mind and in heart to be successful in learning. I often feel that with children who are struggling, parents are often looking for someone to blame, and the easiest way for the finger to point is towards the teacher. When teachers share the difficult news with parents, parents need to trust that the teacher is concerned with the child's ability to be successful and thrive in the SCHOOL environment."

T-R-U-**S**-T
Select a focus.

Unfortunately, the small percentage of teachers who have failed parents' trust stand out more than the ones who keep and maintain parents' trust. That lack of confidence in teachers as a whole is neither the parents' fault nor the teachers', it is how we are programmed as human beings. The question is, on which group are you going to set your focus?

We seem drawn to focus on the few negative things in our lives rather than the many wonderful things that we have. Isn't it easier to dwell on the one person you hate at work rather than think about the dozens of others you get along with just fine? Women, do you find yourself focused on the parts of your body that you dislike rather the parts that are beautiful? When in a struggling relationship, isn't it easier to think about the negative things of the other person rather than all of the positive characteristics? Even when you look at the celebrities, who get the most press? Is it the put-together, beautiful celebrities who have it all, or the once put-together, beautiful celebrities who crash and burn?

While the small percentage of untrustworthy educators are getting more attention and publicity, the rest of teachers, the majority, continue to do their job and work for the success of the students. Most of the teachers your child will have are caring individuals who have studied for many years to do the one thing they are passionate about-*teach*. Of all people, parents are the ones who can fully understand that impacting others with skills that they will be able to do forever is more rewarding than any amount of money. The best and most talented teachers see their student's success as the reward for their efforts. Those great teachers are the ones who will always be searching for the right words, the right lesson, the right exercise that will help their students succeed. Great teachers don't see obstacles, they see challenges they must work around and through.

> "Trust that the teacher just wants to help, listen to what he sees in the class-room, and use it to further understand your child."

I was given a student one year who came in barely able to hold a pencil let alone write his name. But like most young children, he was anxious to learn and willing to work. It took a lot of attention, time, and help from the parents, but we slowly began to see more and more "aha" moments. By the end of the school year he was writing 3-5 sentences as well as writing his first and last name. The only word I can think of to describe what I felt for that student is joy. I would much rather live a life that allows me to have that feeling of joy as opposed to the feeling of happiness of getting a large paycheck each month.

My words could easily be repeated a million times over by teachers across the country. Forces of teachers are in the trenches everyday working for our country's future. My hope is that with awareness people will see the multitude of teachers who are quality individuals. However, do not ignore the negative situations you may run into occasionally. If you have experienced a bad situation, I hope that you and your child can overcome and rise above it. When you get that placement card of your child's future teacher, start trusting. Like one principal said, "Give us a chance and we'll shine for you."

T-R-U-S-**T**
The untold issues.

If you watch a certain TV show regularly, you develop your own perspective about the actors and directors as well the overall show. I have one particular morning show that I love, and since I am already at school by the time it airs I record it to my DVR. This has become a habit since college, and it's gotten to the point where I feel like I know the co-hosts personally. However, no matter how many years I've watched the show, my perspective stays the same unless I get to go behind the scenes.

One year, when visiting New York, my husband and I did just that. My husband, Chase, graciously waited hours in line for me to see the show that I've watched since college. Once inside the building we walked onto the set taking in all of the cameras, props, and cue cards. We even got to meet the co-hosts right before the show. Once the show started it was so interesting to see how what I see on TV comes to fruition. From the small set (which looks spacious on TV) to the interactions between commercials, I had a whole new perspective of my favorite morning show.

In teaching there is also "behind the scene" information that does not always get told to the parents. Sometimes it is information that is required to be confidential and sometimes it is information that is just not necessary to divulge. Just knowing that there are untold issues that can be affecting your child should make you trust your child's teacher even more. There are three main "behind the scenes" issues that could be affecting your child in the classroom.

#1 Classroom issues

The medical world is very aware of the HIPAA (Health Insurance Portability and Accountability Act) privacy rule, which protects information that could lead to a patient's identity. The rule requires that, outside of work, medical professionals are not allowed to talk about any information that could lead someone to identify a patient. Teachers are also required to be very careful about what we say to parents about other students and parents. Of course, parents have a right to know what is going on with *their* child in the classroom, but the discipline, behavior, and parent involvement of other students are not open for discussion. For example, if I had two students who just did not get along and I got an e-mail from one of the parents asking me about the punishments of the other child, I would have to explain that since it was someone else's child, it was their information. I can, however, tell the parents what I as a teacher was doing to help the situation, and how *their* child was doing in the process.

If you find yourself in a situation like this, first just trust that the classroom rules are fair. The teacher is doing his/her best to treat all students equally. It is our job and it is what we are trained to do. Second, be thankful that you and your own information is safe. After all if the teachers can't talk about other students and parents then you can trust that you and your child are not being talked about either.

#2 Diagnosing your child

During conferences, teachers must say everything we need to say to parents in a brief, respectful, and professional manner. A teachers' words could easily be interpreted a number of different ways if not said in the right manner especially in an era where race, religion, and learning disabilities are such touchy subjects. Part of our training as teachers involves not only how to conference with parents in a politically correct, unbiased, and open-minded manner, but also how to teach that way as well.

Since conferences are designed to focus around your child there are little to no constrictions about the information we can tell the parents. One example of the few constrictions, however, is that teachers are not allowed to diagnose students with ADD, ADHD, or anything of the kind. We are not doctors and can get in grave legal trouble if we tell parents their child has a learning disability. What you can do as a parent is listen to what the teacher says during the conference. If you repeatedly hear the symptoms of a learning disability in what the teacher sees in the classroom, then take the initiative and take your child to see a pediatrician. When at the pediatrician, mention some of the phrases that the teacher used – very active, difficult to settle down, hard to focus – so that the doctor has some idea to guide him. Notice that I used the word "repeatedly." If your child has a bad day or even week, it does not mean he has a problem. But if you do hear the same symptoms and issues from the teacher or numerous teachers then take the next step. Then if your child is diagnosed, you can talk with her teacher later about what can be done in the classroom to help your child succeed. In the end, trust that the teacher has the best interest of your child in mind and will tell you everything you need to know to help your child succeed in the classroom.

#3 Pressure from the administration, county, and government

I mentioned in chapter 4 about the stress that standardized testing has put on the administration, teachers, students, and even parents. In order for the school to get substantial funding, the teachers must successfully teach the information, and the students must perform well. Much like your boss who has requirements and goals for you, the states

and cities have requirements for us as educators. Most of the requirements keep teachers working hard and updated on strategies.

Even though these teacher requirements could be affecting your
child (by adding to their education or taking time away from it) most
teachers would much rather spend their time telling you about your
child not this extra *stuff*. As a result, this information will most likely
stay behind the scenes. If you are curious, though, and want to know
what your state is doing in the education world, just ask! Most likely, the
teacher will be more than happy to share his/her opinion!

As you can see, trusting your child's teacher comes in all shapes and
sizes but at the root of it all is one thing-effort. That means effort from
parents and teachers working together to build a relationship in order to
trust. I promise you the effort is worth it because once that trust is built
you can have a peace of mind knowing that your child is at school with
a great person.

Chapter 9

Know your child's learning style

"Teachers are our second parents and also directors of our future."
~High school student

My social studies class in elementary school required that we know the location of all the states in the United States of America. I knew right away the correct location of California, Florida, Texas, New York and other states with a unique shape. However, I consistently incorrectly labeled the states that were similar in shape and size. My parents had the idea to buy me a wooden puzzle of the United States of America. I had fun taking the puzzle apart and putting it back together many times. As a result, I was finally able to label all the states correctly. Thank you mom and dad! Now that I am a teacher, I understand why it finally "clicked" for me. My learning style is *visual* and the puzzle helped me process and learn the layout of each state.

A learning style is how a person processes, receives, and learns information. It is basically a processing style. How children listen, follow directions, and retain information is influenced by their learning style. When parents know the learning style of their children, they can focus on their strengths so that the children can perform tasks to the best of their ability. The individuality of the child's style will be evident as parents observe and study what works for their child. Knowing the learning style of a student is imperative to lessen the frustration of the student's learning experience and expectations. It is important to work with children's natural bend as they learn in order to facilitate their success. My purpose in this chapter is to introduce you to the basic characteristics of each style so that you can begin discovering the learning style of

"When parents know the learning style of their children, they can focus on their strengths so that the children can perform tasks to the best of their ability."

your child. Parents who educate themselves in this area will be better equipped to implement the best practices designed specifically for their child. Educators see each learning style in their classrooms every school year. Success for their child is in the heart of every parent. It will benefit the child and advance her success to know her learning style. Some children are strong in one category and some are a blend of many styles. As teachers we see three basic learning styles in the classroom.

Three Basic Learning Styles

The first learning style is the *visual learner*. This learner does best when shown how to do something visually. Maps, diagrams, DVD's, and charts are all great tools for the visual learner. Visual learners think in words or pictures. They like organization because clutter is a visual stressor to them. Color-coded notebooks and directions are a tremendous help to the visual learner. People with photographic memories are generally visual learners because they take a picture of what they are learning. The visual learners need to see what it is they are learning.

The second learning style is the *auditory learner*. This learner catches his information by listening. The use of music, conversation, books on tape, and verbal lecture are great methods to use for this learner. In fact, the auditory learner does better with music going on in the background because it helps him concentrate. It helps this learner to go over information for a test or quiz orally. When memory work is needed, it helps the auditory learner to put information to music. This learner catches information by hearing what he is learning.

The third learning style is the *tactile-kinesthetic learner.* Tactile refers to touch. Kinesthetic refers to motion. This learner does best when she can touch and move around in the learning environment. The use of white boards, chalkboards, and math manipulatives are wonderful tools for the tactile-kinesthetic learner. This learner would love it if the teacher gave her shaving cream on her desk to practice writing her letters or practice simple math. Often this learner is seen as a challenge for the teacher in a structured classroom because she finds it hard to sit still and she wants to be up and moving around the room. This learner does well counting on her fingers for math. They do well in athletics later on in school and any activity that involves movement. Courses that are designed to have hands-on instruction are perfect for these learners. They need to touch and move when learning.

Learning Styles in the Classroom

Each student has a learning style. Each teacher also has a learning style. The classroom environment will reflect the learning style of the teacher. My classroom reflects that I am a visual learner. I use bright and colorful visuals. I organize my paperwork for my classes in color-coordinated folders. I am also partly a tactile-kinesthetic learner so much of my instructional time uses hands-on lessons. My curriculum allows lab work, which allows students to get out of their seats. My daughter, Tiffany, is a tactile-kinesthetic learner so she does a lot of movement with her students. They do the Macarena as they say the months of the year, they exercise as they count by 2's, 5's, and10's, and they make up motions to remember sight words (common words that are found in basic reading).

During the course of a child's education, he is likely to encounter teachers with all three learning styles. The parent who is knowledgeable of learning styles will be able to help their child make adjustments to teacher's styles especially when it is a different style from their own. It may be a challenge at times, but being an informed parent regarding the learning styles will assist in planning solutions.

Parents can design ways to help their child function in the classroom with his/her particular learning style. Also when parents sense that their child is struggling in a learning situation, they can make the necessary adjustments. For example, if a parent has a tactile-kinesthetic learner, they can teach the child self discipline habits to stay in his seat during class. Role-playing with your child is a great way to practice different methods to assist your child in classroom conduct. It is a positive thing for children to learn how to adapt to different environments because certain expectations are essential in the classroom setting. Parents of a visual learner can identify a subject with a certain color when buying book covers or notebooks for a particular subject. This will help in organizing the visual learner. Parents of the auditory learner can find books on tape outside of the classroom for their learner to review.

"Students thrive when they learn in their own natural way."

Students thrive when they learn in their own natural way. As a result, a movement in teaching called "differentiated instruction" encourages teachers to teach to the individual student. There are classes, books, and websites full of tips for teachers to learn how to produce lessons that engage each student's level and learning style. Parents have the benefit of just having to know *your* children's learning style rather than 30 children's learning styles. During homework time with your child, incorporate strategies that fit her learning style. Overtime we know you will see improvement.

Personality types in the classroom

I was taking attendance one morning in first period class when one of my seniors spoke up and asked me if I take a "happy pill" every morning. It made me laugh. I quickly realized that the student asking me had a melancholy temperament. She was also not a morning person. Just for fun I assured her that I would absolutely stop being pleasant and happy. No more of this smiling or laughing! Immediately my extraverted students quieted her and announced that they like it and wanted me to keep smiling and being happy. She ended up smiling too.

I have learned to celebrate the differences in people, and that includes my students. I have fun getting to know each student and their unique personalities. As their teacher, I can do the best I can to adjust my expectations and interaction with them when I pay attention to the way they are "wired." Every individual has a distinctive personality that touches people around him or her each day. Each day when I walk into my classroom I observe an array of personality-related behaviors. It has helped me as an educator to be aware of personality traits. In the classroom environment, it is important for the teacher to recognize these differences so that children can be themselves within the guidelines of the school. Each personality type has a positive and a negative quality. The personality of a student influences how he learns, so learning these traits helps us understand the child's response to the school setting. Parents can guide their children in a way that will help them respect the classroom by using the positive side of their personalities.

There are 28 different personalities in my classroom each day. It is important for me to get to know this aspect of each student so that I can be sensitive to their needs and how to relate them. There are ways that I can draw on their personalities to present my lessons. When we are reading out loud in class, my extraverted students are the first to raise their hands and volunteer. When I give an assignment that involves artistic expression, my melancholy students are generally the most creative. The students who have leadership personalities are my go-to-students when I need participants to role-play as part of the lesson. My shy and quiet students are wonderful if I need papers sorted. All day long I interact and handle personality types in the classroom. I must have an appreciation and knowledge of each type in order to facilitate the success of my students.

If you would like a more professional view of your child's personality, there are many personality tests available for parents to choose. Several companies now require their employees to take personality tests in order to learn the person's strengths as well as where to place individuals in the company. Many counselors also encourage personality tests to help the relationships between husbands and wives or children and parents. I would not be concerned about this activity "labeling" anyone. It is a wonderful tool to give parents an idea of how their child functions. I find it invaluable when understanding the actions of my students and also my own children. The tests define terms, explain variables, and give practical explanation of behaviors. If my paycheck allowed, I would give my students a personality test every year to help me better learn their strengths. I would love it, then, if parents informed me that their child took a personality test and were willing to share some of the information. There are a variety of personality tests that I have found useful but one of the most well-known is Myers-Briggs. Do your research and find one that works for *your* family.

Going beyond the Learning Styles and Personality Types

What to do when there is a learning disability present.

In most cases children are diagnosed with a learning disability before they even set foot in a classroom. What we also know is that if you are a parent of a child diagnosed with a learning disability then you have probably already bought the books, read the articles, and talked to the doctors to help you understand your child's needs. Along with the doctors and scholars who have already provided you with help, we hope to provide another area of help. Teachers are also a group of professionals who are comfortable and trained to work with students who have learning disabilities. For this section we talked *specifically* to teachers who specialize in working alongside students with learning disabilities to discover what strategies they use in their classrooms.

Our goal is to encourage you that even if your child has been diagnosed with a learning disability it does not make him/her unreachable, we just have to find the right strategy. After reading about the learning styles above you might already recognize one or two learning styles that might work for your child. We want to encourage you to practice using the learning styles as well as use some of the strategies from the specialized teachers we are about to mention. We covered the areas that we see most often in the classroom: dyslexia, ADD/ADHD, Autism, Asperger's Syndrome, and Speech and Language Problems.

Dyslexia

What is it?

A dyslexia specialist from Texas described dyslexia as the following: "The main thing to know is a student who struggles with dyslexia means that there is a glitch in the neurological wiring of dyslexics that makes reading extremely difficult for him/her. To understand what sorts of glitches we're talking about, it helps to know a little about how the brain works. The brain is broken into two hemispheres:

Right Side: more attuned to analyzing spatial cues.
Left Side: particularly adept at processing language
Within the left side there are three areas:

- Left inferior frontal gyros-the 'phoneme producer' which includes saying things out loud and analysis of phonemes (the smallest sounds that make up words).
- Left parieto-temporal area-the 'word analyzer' which analyzes words more thoroughly by pulling out syllables and phonemes and linking letters to their sounds.
- Left occipito-temporal area-the 'automatic detector' which is the ability to build repertoire and enables readers to recognize familiar words on sight. Eventually this area begins to dominate.

For dyslexia students the glitches prevent them from easily accessing the *word analyzer* and the *automatic detector.* These students compensate for the problem by over activating the *phoneme producer.* So when reading the word *cat*, the brain will focus on the individual sounds (phonemes) in no particular order; making the word *cat* look like *tca*."

What can parents do at home?

We know that the human brain is receptive to instruction, otherwise, practice would never make perfect. Unfortunately there are no "quick fixes" but below are some strategies you can use when teaching your child.

1. Emphasize the same core elements: practice manipulating phonemes, building vocabulary, increasing comprehension and improving the fluency of reading.

2. Before we can focus on learning to read sentences, we have to teach them to recognize sounds, then syllables, then words, and sentences. This child requires lots of practice and repetition.

3. Teach tricks or rules for reading: for instance, the magic e at the end of words that makes a vowel say is name (make, cute, bike).

4. A dyslexic child might have difficulty in organizing his or her day-to-day tasks and learning skills. As a parent one cannot simply tell such a child to clean up her room. They should be specific: for instance: pick up the clothes and put them in the laundry basket or hang them, pick up papers, put away the shoes and put them in the closet).

5. Dyslexic children tend to have a short attention span and are easily distracted by too much noise or too much going on around them. Parents can help by removing all distractions and by keeping the room fairly quiet when the child is at work.

Autism/ Asperger's Syndrome

What is it?

Autism is a general term used to describe a developmental disability caused by a neurological disorder and affects an individual's functioning of the brain. Unfortunately autism does not have a nice, neat list of symptoms because there is such a wide range of them. Luckily, as a result of many years of research and extensive study some similarities have been found, so that it is now possible to make some basic general statements about what children with autism are like as a group. Asperger's Syndrome is a high performing form of autism with similar symptoms focusing more on the lack of development in social skills.

- Lack of development in social skills
- Conflict in speech, language, and communication
- Abnormal relationships to objects and events
- Unusual responses to sensory stimulation
- Developmental delays and differences
- Begins during infancy or childhood

Today, it is estimated that one in every 150 children is diagnosed with autism. As we became more aware of autism in our country, so are our institutions which have focused on educating teachers in how to work alongside students with autism. Also, with time, more strategies are being found succesful to help students complete tasks in a fluid manner.

What can parents do at home?

1. Children with autism thrive in a predictable routine. Develop a schedule that works for your family and do your best to stick to it. If you have a busy lifestyle, choose a few of the most important parts of your day that you can make consistent. For example: wake-up, breakfast, homework, dinner, and bedtime.

2. Reduce distractions visually. Children with autism are easily distracted or over stimulated. Limit the clutter in your house, especially in areas where your child spends the most time.

3. Reduce distractions audibly. Give directions one step at a time. After each direction, allow your child time to process the information.

4. Use clear language, short sentences, and simple vocabulary to increase comprehension. If your child still does not comprehend your sentence, then reword the sentence and try again.

5. Have a "safe" place that your child can go when overwhelmed. This may be his bedroom or a quiet sitting room with classical music being played.

ADD/ADHD

What is it?

Attention Deficit/Hyperactivity Disorder is a neurological disorder characterized by lack of attention, impulsive behavior, and possible hyperactivity. However, after reading that description, most would agree that all children at some time will struggle with one or more of those areas. There is a difference between developmentally appropriate behaviors compared to behaviors that are so persistent that they affect a child's everyday function. As a kindergarten teacher, Tiffany sees many of these characteristics in her students; however, she seldom considers ADHD an option because the students are still adjusting to the classroom environment, learning the rules, and how to function in a large group setting. Having occasional mannerisms of inattention, impulsivity, and hyperactivity are developmentally appropriate. It is not until a little later in a child's school journey that doctors and parents should consider ADHD an option. Teachers will never be able to diagnose your child with ADHD, so the best option if you believe your child might have ADHD is to listen to what the teachers see at school, join it with what you see at home, and then discuss it with your pediatrician. Your pediatrician will be the professional who can diagnose and assist if your child has ADD or ADHD.

What can parents do at home?

1. For studying at home, find a relatively uncluttered, quiet place to focus. Have a set pattern of a study time developed for your child.

2. Body language is key. Children with ADD or ADHD are very observant to body language. If you get angry or frustrated, walk away until you are ready to speak in a calm manner.

3. Use positive reinforcement to encourage good behavior to be repeated. This could look as simple as giving your child an M&M every time he displays a positive behavior like studying straight for 20 minutes or putting clothes in the dirty hamper.

4. Repetition, repetition, repetition. Children with ADD or ADHD thrive in environments that follow a consistent routine. The repetition enables the child to become familiar with what is expected of him, and what he will have to do during the day. In a routine, less outside influences are present to "throw off" the child's day. For example, one teacher who is an ADD specialist suggested packing your child's lunch everyday. The numerous choices of the lunch line can cause for distraction or confusion for the child.

5. Consider an outside tutor. Look for a college student or teacher who is skilled and willing to tutor your child. This allows you, the parent, to be rested and ready to handle life at home with your child.

Speech and Language

What is it?

Speech and language disabilities cover a wide variety of issues. Speech disorders usually involve characteristics such as the inability to produce speech sounds correctly and fluently or the child may have problems with his or her voice. Language disorders may involve trouble understanding others, or sharing thoughts, ideas, and feelings completely.

What can parents do at home?
1. Use clear language, short sentences, and simple vocabulary to increase comprehension.

2. Read to your child as often as possible to enhance vocabulary, language skills, and sequence of events.

3. Encourage your child to listen to books on tape or simple, repetitive songs to reinforce correct speech patterns.

4. Practice is key. For example, if your child struggles with the /th/ sound, emphasize the sound in your speech, talk about your tongue/lip placement when saying the sound, and encourage your child to repeat words that include the sound. Do not expect perfection but be ready to praise effort even if it falls short of the goal.

5. Give your child time to listen when you give her instructions. Make sure you have her attention, and encourage verbal response to the instructions.

Every child is unique in how she learns, loves, and communicates. In order to relate and work with your child on a day-to-day basis, the strategies that we mentioned in this chapter are essential. Study your child, and then be willing to make some adjustments yourself. Relationships take effort but the effort is worth it. You are the expert on your child.

Chapter

10

Parents are the common denominator

I asked my kindergarten students:

"What is the best thing your parents have taught you?"

Here were their responses:

"How to tie my shoe."

"How to play soccer."

"How to pray."

"How to share."

There is no doubt that parents teach their children more things than can be counted. From how to talk to how to drive a car, parents are constantly teaching, modeling, and helping their children. You are the most important factor in your child's life because you are the common denominator.

It didn't take me long as an educator to recognize the importance and influence parents have with their children, which is why when I heard of one idea that would utilize the love and knowledge of my students' parents, I jumped on the chance. It was the idea of having a get-to-know-you conference during the first couple weeks of school. At first the idea sounded bizzare because as a kindergarten teacher the words "first couple weeks of school" could easily be defined with the 3C's:

1. Chaos
2. Crying (from both parents and students)
3. Confusion (from both parents and students).

One year, however, I worked extra hard to get everything in order so I could at least attempt to have the get-to-know-you conferences. The idea appealed to me because the conference is designed for parents to help the teacher get to know their child *before* a relationship with the student is even developed. All I needed to do as a teacher was sit back and listen to the person who loved, knew, and cherished my new student the most-their parents. I can honestly say that even though it meant several late nights, more questions, and some extra tears, it was entirely worth it. To this day, I can hardly imagine starting the school year without it.

What I did was ask 4 simple questions to each of the parents:

1. What are your child's academic strengths/weaknesses?
2. What are your child's personal strengths/weaknesses?
3. What is your child passionate about in life?
4. What behavior strategies do you do at home that works with your child?

What I received was a wealth of knowledge that would not only help enhance my abilities as a teacher, but it benefited the overall dynamics of my classroom. No book, college course, or expert could have helped me as much as the words from those parents. Usually it takes a teacher weeks, sometimes months, to find out the answers to those questions. Even if the parents didn't know an exact answer to the question, it was still nice to see them glow as they talked about their precious little one. While I knew that the information was beneficial from the start, I was still pleasantly surprised to find myself using the information frequently throughout the school year. When a child ran out of ideas to write about, I reminded him of one of the "passions" his parents had mentioned. When a child began to push the limit behaviorally I looked to see what behavior strategies worked at home and implemented them. And when a child started to lose interest I looked at her personal strengths and designed a classroom job just for her. Something as simple as listening to a parent enabled me to become a more personal, efficient, and improved teacher, and it made our classroom a better classroom.

When someone asked me why I thought the get-to-know-you conference helped so much it didn't take long to realize that it worked because the parents were involved. If our nation's goal is to create classrooms that teach to the individual student, we have to use parents as the number one resource. There is nothing better than a parent who takes a stand and turns off the TV, puts away the video games, reads to their child, helps with homework, and attends parent-teacher conferences. Responsibility for our children's education must begin at home.

> "There is nothing better than a parent who takes a stand and turns off the TV, puts away the video games, reads to their child, helps with homework, and attends parent-teacher conferences."

That is the whole intention of this book: *parents are the key.* And, since this is the closing advice on the list of things teachers want parents to know, we chose to share the more personal tips for your child at each educational level: elementary, middle, and high school. On top of the general question we asked teachers at the beginning of the book, we also asked them, "What skills, behaviors, or manners do you feel are most important for students in *your* grade level?" We chose a top 10 for each grade level, and as you will see teachers in more than one grade level repeated a couple of the same guidelines.

No matter what age level your child is at currently, I recommend that you read all of the advice below. It is never too late to start implementing strategies that will help with your child's school participation and, if your child is young, it will provide a look as to what you can expect for the future.

Elementary School: SCHOOL 101

While it may not appear so at first, the school journey prepares us for similar experiences in our adult life. For example, before starting your major classes in college you must first take courses that set a foundation for what you will later learn in detail. These core classes set a foundation for the rest of your time in college. You develop a schedule, you learn how to interact with professors, and you learn how to manage your workload. Since this experience is new, you might even seek help from a tutor or an upperclassman. After all, this is just the start and you want to get it right.

During the school journey, elementary school is where the foundation is built. The skills learned during this time are the building blocks for what will be developed and experienced later in middle and high school. It is also the time when your child needs the most guidance and help. Your role as a parent becomes that of a *tutor*. A tutor is one who is readily available to model and explain a new concept. Since most things are new to your child at this age, elementary school will probably take the most of your time as a parent; however, if your time is spent right it will help immensely in years to come when your child is older and having to do more on her own. Below are several skills that will help you in setting a firm foundation for your child.

1.Read with your child. Reading with your child regularly not only enhances your child's attitude towards reading, but it also provides "together-time" that results in a special bond only a parent and child can share. Additionally, reading helps enhance vocabulary, fluency, spelling, and creativity. Since reading not only benefits your child socially but mentally, you want to ensure that the moments spent reading are positive ones. Below are some helpful strategies to use that will help make reading with your child a positive experience.

Create a comfortable routine: Find a quiet spot to snuggle up with your child and a good book. Whether it's 15 minutes every night before bed, or once a week, your "together-time" can go a long way in getting your child interested in books.

Choose an appropriate book: Many teachers use the "five-finger rule." Open up the book to any page and begin reading. Every time your child comes to a word he/she does not know have him hold up one finger. If five fingers are held up before the bottom of the page, the book is probably too difficult for your child. No fingers means the book is most likely too easy, and 2-3 fingers means the book should be challenging but readable.

Be a model example: In order for your child to become a fluent reader, he needs to hear great models who read with inflection. Make reading fun by using funny voices or impersonating animal sounds. In your spare time, choose to read a book that interests you. Seeing you read shows your child that books are interesting at all ages.

Use sound strategies to tackle new words: If your child is a beginning reader, read a sentence from the book (pointing to each word at a time) and then have him repeat the same sentence. Doing so will help him recognize some common words as well as hear the steady flow of reading out loud. As your child emerges as a reader, ask her to "sound out" unknown words. Stretch out the sounds that each individual letter makes and then blend them together to say the word (i.e. d-o-g=dog).

Ask comprehension questions: While it is important to know how to read, it is equally important to understand what is being read. Throughout a story ask your child questions to ensure that he understands the story. For example:

- About the characters: "Who is this story about?" "What do you think he/she is thinking right now?" "How would you describe the character (i.e. kind, mean, mysterious)?"
- Make predictions: "What do you think will happen next?" "How will the character feel if that happens?"
- Encourage opinions: "Do you think that was the best choice?" What would you have done if you were a character in the book?"
- Summarize the information: "What was that story all about?" "Did you learn anything from the story?"

Give support and encouragement: Encourage your child to figure out new words but always supply the word before she gets too frustrated.

Praise your child for working so hard to finish a story or sound out a word. Enjoy looking and talking about the illustrations (which can also be used to help read the sentences).

Make reading continuous. Don't stop reading to your children once they've learned how to read on their own. Continue your read-alouds in order to enhance your child's vocabulary and exposure to new books.

2. Use everyday materials to learn math skills. From stuffed animals to cereal, almost anything around the house can be used to create a math problem. Practice adding by joining together your fruit snacks with your child's. Learn subtracting by letting your child "take away" some of your beads during a craft. Understand dividing by learning how to "share" a snack with a group of people so that everyone has the same amount. Use objects around the house or store to identify shapes and patterns. The activities are endless. All you have to do is take the time.

3. Practice money. Money is one of the most practical math skills learned in school. It is something that your children will use almost everyday for the rest of their lives. Experiencing money is a wonderful skill for elementary school children. Use any and every opportunity possible to allow your child practice with money from merely identifying the coins and bills to counting enough money to purchase a soda.

Encourage your children to save their money. A popular strategy several of my students' parents used was giving their child a "give," "save," and "spend" piggy bank. Any time the children received money, they would distribute the money equally among the three piggy banks. Once a desired amount is reached, the money was given to a chosen charity, spent on a desired toy, or saved for something special in the future. This strategy is beneficial for several areas of math including counting, sorting, identifying, and comparing.

4. Give your child a journal. Becoming a fluent reader often helps a child become a better writer and vice versa. Journaling is one of the simplest but most beneficial things you can have your child do at home.

It enables the student to write whatever he/she desires without anyone looking, judging, or requiring a certain amount. Your child can make up imaginary stories, write about a past experiences, or draw pictures from a favorite book. Make the journal special. You can give it as a gift or have your child pick it out at the store. The point is to develop ownership; this journal is *theirs*.

5. Establish your child's fine motor skills. On the surface it may not seem that stringing a necklace with beads would have anything to do with academics; however, activities such as stringing beads, playing with play dough, and painting a picture can help your child with her handwriting. Fine motor skills can be defined as the cooperation of small muscle movements that occur in the fingers and hands and are usually in coordination with the eyes. Developing these muscles at a young age will greatly help your child with everything from tying a shoe, developing neat handwriting, and typing.

6. Create positive homework habits early. If positive homework habits are developed in elementary school they will set a foundation for similar habits in middle and high school as well. Below are the guidelines to creating a thriving, homework environment.

- Establish a routine and give homework its own special time and place.
- Map out a plan for the amount of homework there is, and make sure to break periodically so as not to overwhelm your child.
- For optimal concentration, provide an environment that is well lit and reasonably quiet.
- Be available as a resource but encourage independent problem solving.
- Kids love to hear that they are doing well, so be vocal with your praise (especially near the end of the school year when laziness tends to increase).
- In the end, know that a healthy balance between school and free time is beneficial. Encourage your child to play outside or read a

favorite book; doing so will not only provide a break for the mind, but it will also help your child develop valuable time-management skills.

7. Practice manners used in groups. Attending some sort of daycare, camp, or small group setting will help provide an environment for your child to learn many social skills needed for school such as sharing, getting along with others, following rules, behavior expectations, and respect toward others concerning when to talk and when to listen. These environments also provide a way to learn and get used to a set schedule of work time along with restroom breaks and snack time. Some other very important manners that teachers suggested were saying "please" and "thank you," looking at an adult when being spoken to, and sitting down to eat.

8. Encourage independence and hard work. In order to teach personal responsibility, students need to start at home by doing tasks like making their beds, getting dressed on their own, and cleaning up toys. If they are doing these things at home, the behaviors will carry into the classroom setting. It will take more time and patience but the rewards are well worth it! As one teacher stated, "Babying children is such a disservice and hinders children from reaching their full potential academically." The ability of your child may be different from others of the same age. Encourage your child to try something several times before moving on to another skill. Children are very capable if given the chance. It is amazing what a little responsibility and encouragement can to for a child's personal growth!

9. Talk with your child. Carrying on a conversation with your child increases his oral and language skills. A kindergarten teacher notes, "I remember sitting in the car (not watching a DVD) and singing songs, counting, telling stories with my parents, having them explain to me where they are going, and what we were doing. The TV, radio, and videos cannot and will not replace crucial interactions that develop vocabulary, social, and behavioral skills that prepare a child for the school and life setting."

10. Be involved with your child's school. Understanding the environment where your children spend 8 hours of their days will give you more credibility to carry on similar strategies at home. Schools provide many opportunities for parents to familiarize themselves with the school environment such as volunteering in the classrooms, Curriculum Nights, Open Houses, and Parent-Teacher Conferences. Choose which events you are able to attend and make them your priority. If you cannot attend an event, ask the teacher to send home any information that you missed.

Middle School: Working in an internship

You are in your senior year of college now. You have chosen your field of expertise and you are ready to practice what you've learned from your core classes. You begin an internship with someone who is experienced and can be a guide while letting you practice on your own, too. You feel ready for independence but you know your skills are not perfect yet. Hopefully with your mentor's help you will learn.

Like an intern, middle school students must now practice the skills, strategies, and knowledge that they have required in elementary school but with less help. Although students in middle school appear ready for more responsibility, they still need guidance. Being a parent of a middle school student will probably not require as much physical time as elementary school. Instead your time is spent assisting and your role, as a parent, becomes that of a *mentor*. A great mentor is someone who is able to find a balance between helping too much versus complete independence. A mentor remains available to help but knows that some of the best lessons are learned through experience. The following provides advice of how to maintain this difficult balance.

1. Teach organization. About 99% of the middle school teachers I polled included this advice in their answer. As one teacher stated, "Organization is the key to success in middle school." Below are some tips straight from the mouths of middle school teachers about how to stay organized:

Use an agenda or calendar to help keep track of assignments and after school activities. The transition from elementary school to middle school is a huge one. The biggest change is the amount of homework and assignments that your child is responsible for. One middle school teacher noted, "Every class, every day, students should write down what is expected (homework or no homework). Teachers will write all homework assignments on the board and on their class websites, too." Encourage your child to write down the due dates as well. Check your child's agenda on a daily basis to ensure that assignments are being completed and upcoming tests are being studied for. Some schools even have a homework hotline that parents can call for any further questions. If your child participates in after school activities, write those in the calendar as well. Doing so will limit questions about what they have to do, and they can start taking responsibility of their own schedule.

"Organization is the key to success in middle school."

Be prepared with the correct supplies. In elementary school, teachers usually work with one group of children the entire day, which means that supplies (like pencils, papers, and crayons) are a little easier to provide. In middle school, teachers have hundreds of students pass through their doors each day making it difficult to offer the correct supplies. Start each school year by looking at the teacher's supply list. If there is a specific item on the list, there is a reason. If you cannot find the item, ask the teacher or a fellow parent where they obtained theirs. Middle school students should be taking notes in class on a daily basis making pencils the most required item. Encourage your child to start each day with a pencil. As one teacher said, "You don't have to tell your children to put their shoes on to go to school, they just do it. By middle school the same should be true of having a pencil."

Inform your child about locker protocol. Before your children starts middle school, get them a lock for their locker so they can practice the combination. One teacher encouraged parents, "Sometime during the first month of school, check your child's locker. An organized locker can speed your child to class while a messy locker can be a source of endless frustration. Parents know what it's like trying to find a shoe in their child's room when they should have left for the recital 20 minutes ago. Kids visit their locker 5-6 times a day, so frustration can quickly escalate from not being able to lay their hands on homework they know they did."

2. Model how to type and research on the computer. Many of the assignments in middle school require the use of a computer. Even if your children are familiar with computers, they still need to know tricks like typing without looking at the keyboard, using a search engine, and making sure information is credible. Typing and researching is a learned skill and must be practiced. Your child can practice typing by writing e-mails to relatives and friends. If a question arises about a certain topic, encourage your child to research the answer.

3. Continue reading. Even though your children can read on their own, continue your "together-time" by talking about books or reading aloud. Encourage your child to read for entertainment not just for school. One teacher suggested starting a family book circle where all members read the same book and discuss the book together.

4. Provide opportunities for responsibility. Middle school students are given more responsibility in the classroom, so any additional opportunity at home is beneficial practice. Give your child opportunities to be responsible at home with household chores, making the grocery list, writing a birthday card, and researching things to do in your own city or on vacation. If your children have difficulty being accountable, start small and give them opportunities to succeed. Being successful a couple of times will help encourage them to continue.

5. Start saving. As discussed in the elementary school advice, continue familiarizing your child with the saving, spending, and giving of money. As children get older, the "toys" get bigger and more expensive. Encourage your children to start saving for things they might like in the future (i.e. a car, bike, or video game system). Doing so will not only help the parents financially but it will also enable your children to have ownership of their belongings. When a person has ownership of an item, he is more likely to take care of it and treat it with respect.

6. Start your day with brain food. Providing your children with the nutrients they need will help them power through an 8-hour school day, stay alert, and participate in extra curricular activities. Make an effort to fill your child's breakfast with proteins, antioxidants, and Omega-3 Fatty acids-all of which many doctors have labeled "brain foods." Skipping the first meal of the day could hinder academic performance and interfere with a child's learning at school. Below is a list of simple, quick meal ideas to implement brain foods into your morning routine.

- Sprinkle oatmeal with flaxseed, honey, and dried cranberries.
- Top cereal with cinnamon, almonds, and sliced peaches.
- Top granola with low fat yogurt, cinnamon, and berries.
- Cook sausage patties (turkey or regular) ahead of time and reheat them during the week.
- Blend fruit, yogurt, protein powder, and flaxseed oil to make a delicious smoothie. Accompany with a slice of wheat toast buttered and toasted with cinnamon-sugar.
- Scramble organic eggs and mix with some vegetables. Serve over whole-wheat toast.
- For snacks, work in as many fruits and vegetables as possible. Make your own trail mixes with nuts, dried fruit, and cereal.

7. Practice positive study habits. If positive study habits were developed early on, all you have to do is continue the routine, but it's never too late to start. If you're starting a new routine, refer back to the positive study habits mentioned above in the elementary school section.

8. Participate in conversations with your child. Your child is now of age where you can converse with him/her about personal ideas, beliefs, and opinions. Conversations will not only help you understand where your child is coming from, but it also allows him to practice appropriate conversation skills such as: knowing how to start a conversation, listening, responding, interacting, and closing a conversation that he can carry on into the adult world. If practiced from early on, the art of conversations can be mastered by the time your child is interviewing for colleges or jobs. If your child happens to ask you a question that you cannot answer, refer back to Mark Twain who said, "I was gratified to be able to answer promptly. I said I didn't know." Merely saying, "I don't know" demonstrates the wonderful fact that we are not perfect creatures who know everything. Learning is an ongoing process. If we knew everything there would be no mystery in life. If you do not know the answer, take the time to look it up with your child.

9. Stay involved in your child's school. Even though your child is older and appears more capable, your time is still needed in their school. To be a successful mentor you must become familiar with the expectations that are required of your child. Make it a priority to attend as many parent-teacher conferences and school functions as your time allows. Showing your support for school activities will demonstrate to your child that they are indeed important.

10. Discover your child's interests. Get your child involved in after school activities that enhance teamwork. Being able to work well with others is a crucial skill for school and life. Get a feel for what your child loves and is passionate about. High school provides a multitude of clubs, opportunities and teams in which your children can participate. Knowing early on what areas they love will help in the decision making later on.

High School: Starting a new job

You've passed your core classes, you managed your way through an internship, and you finally got the job you wanted. You feel confident in your abilities, but you're still getting comfortable with being on your own; on the other hand, you don't feel too alone because your boss is there checking to ensure that deadlines are met, appointments are kept, and that you are giving your best effort.

The good news is, as a parent of a high school student, your role is most like that of a *boss*. While your child is responsible to keep up with deadlines, papers, and assignments, you can oversee their efforts to ensure that everything is running smoothly. You are available to help if needed, but your main job requirement is to manage from a distance. In elementary school your child learned skills,

"In elementary school your child learned the skills, in middle school they practiced them, but in high school they must implement them."

in middle school they practiced them, but in high school they must implement them. The following shows strategies that will enable your children to implement some already learned skills into their daily life. After all, what we truly desire as parents and teachers is to prepare this young generation for a flourishing, independent lifestyle.

1. Everything matters. By saying that "everything matters" in high school does not mean that everything did not count in elementary and middle school. It means that, starting freshman year of high school your child's grades will be looked at either by future colleges or jobs. Consequently the importance of keeping up with deadlines, assignments, and tests is imperative. As you can see, your role as "boss" is much needed.

2. Implement good study habits. No matter if your child is in elementary, middle, or high school, the positive study habits remain the same.

The younger your children learns these skills, the easier they will be able to implement them in high school when they receive loads of work. Refer back to the study habits mentioned in the elementary school section above for clarification.

3. Continue the brain food. The high school schedule is very demanding, so a nutritious breakfast is imperative for your child. Refer back to the middle school section to see the benefits behind a well-balanced breakfast as well as some delicious and simple meal ideas.

4. Provide opportunities for more responsibility. Just like a new employee, your children need to exercise responsibility. The more practice they have, the more opportunities they have to succeed. The responsibility you give your child will be unique to your family's beliefs, finances, and personal situation. Sit down with your child and discuss the responsibilities that fit your family. Do you want your child to work after school or not? Will your child be responsible for buying her own car, or will she be responsible for the upkeep of a current car? Will you provide your child with a credit card and a budget, or will she finance it independently? The options are endless; do what works for you and your family. Most importantly, catch your child doing something well and tell him. If they followed through with a responsibility tell them how proud you are.

5. Encourage your children to pursue their passions. To have passion is one of life's simple pleasures. If your child is so lucky to find a passion, give her the confidence to pursue it because you never know where it will lead. Providing your support will demonstrate that you value your child as a person. Be your child's personal cheerleader.

6. Stay connected with school activities. High school is filled with opportunities to attend everything from sporting events to fundraisers to school plays. Even if your child does not participate in the event, your presence still represents that you appreciate the efforts and hard work of the staff and students involved. Keep in mind that we are all on the same team.

7. Talk with the teachers. High school teachers still need to interact with parents whether your child is struggling or doing well. Inform the teacher if something major in your family occurs. If the teachers are aware of the situation, they can seek the right counsel or even just seat your child next to a helpful student. If there are no problems and your child seems to be doing well, feel open to send the teacher a short e-mail periodically saying, "How's my child doing in your class?" Staying involved demonstrates to your child that school is important.

8. Keep your child accountable. Since elementary school, teachers encourage the teaching of responsibility to children. Now is the time to implement what has been taught and practiced. Keep your children accountable for the responsibilities they hold: assignments, tests, projects, after school activities. Even with your help as a guide, mistakes will happen. Allow your child to live and learn without placing the blame elsewhere.

9. Be a parent not a friend. Remember if you are a parent of a high school student, your role is that of a boss. It is essential for parents to be present and able to set guidelines. You might be labeled as "strict" or "unfair," but what your child does not see is that the guidelines are providing security. For example, imagine if your boss never provided a course of action, checked deadlines, or dealt with office issues. At first it would seem great, but over time you would feel lost and unsure of what exactly was required of you. Similarly, your child needs to know what is expected of him or he will get confused. Your child is not yet completely impendent; he still needs you present.

10. Teach life skills. At the start of college, many of my friends did not know how to perform every day tasks like laundry, balancing a checkbook, or filling out paperwork. Although I didn't appreciate it in high school, I ended up very thankful that my parents took the time to teach me the life skills I needed to get by on my own. It saved me a lot of stress, time, and ruined clothes! As a parent, explain tricks that you use and have found successful. For example, if you have a strategy for doing laundry share it. If you organize your bills a certain way let them know. Laundry, banking, bills, filling out paperwork, insurance, cleaning and cooking are some basic but useful topics that you can discuss with your children before they graduate from high school.

Finally, remember that learning is a continuous journey. Education is a lifelong process of which school is only a small yet important part. You are never too old to learn something new. While on your journey use this book as your guide. Use the words, tips and advice from our nation's teachers that were written specifically to you-*the parent*. Use your love and knowledge to benefit your child's education because you are your child's common denominator in life. You can make a difference in our nation's education system because it all starts somewhere, and that somewhere is you.

Sincerely,

The Teacher

Class Dismissed!

"Class dismissed" are the two favorite words in the vocabulary of every student. Students are delighted to be moving on to their next class or going home for the day. The learning experience for that day is done. Backpacks in tow, the students rush off to their buses, cars, practices, tutorials, or club meetings. The frenzy in a high school hallway at the end of a day is overwhelming! Lockers are slamming, peers are hollering to each other down the hall, and reminders to "Facebook me tonight!" are shouted. In the elementary school, the teachers are focused on one thing-getting their precious students on the right bus. I have a great amount of respect for all the teachers who do carpool lines. I would be a wreck!

But once the dust settles and quiet returns to the hallways, there is someone still in each empty classroom. That person is the teacher. The teacher now has a moment for herself to stop and reflect on the day. She asks herself how things went that day. She wonders if her students "caught" the lessons taught, and if the students will use the material learned for everyday life. But she is not alone. Across America, at the end of the day, teachers want to feel that they have done a good job for their students. It is in the heart of each teacher to facilitate learning each and every day.

To us this book is no different. We are finished writing, and now we look back and reflect. We hope that like our students, the material taught won't stop here. Our hope is that you will use this information and make it a part of your lifestyle. This project started as my daughter's idea because she saw a need for parents and teachers to function well together for the sake of the students. These chapters have been a "classroom" so to speak, where two teachers opened up our world for parents to see and hopefully better understand. Our hope is that you sensed our sincerity to bridge any gaps between parents and teachers. We need one another and so do our amazing students. We care deeply about educating our future generations and making a positive impact on the children we are privileged to educate. There are so many personal rewards in teaching. Teachers have a front row seat to watch the future generation evolve and mature. We want that experience to be outstanding and life changing for each student.

We want to work with the parents to make this happen. Working together will create a positive environment for each child. We all desire to boost the achievement of each student. In closing, we hope that parents know how much we appreciate them. And with that being said *class dismissed!*

Terminology 101

Cheat Sheet of Educational Terms

As a parent, do you ever feel like your child's teacher is speaking a different language? Once they start throwing out terms like "EIP, IEP, and SST" does your brain go into overload? Well, hopefully this "cheat sheet" will be your guide into some of the many terms educators use on a day-to-day basis. And don't worry; even teachers have difficulty remembering all of the terms!

Accreditation: An authorized certification that guarantees that a school is providing high quality education to its students. Schools must maintain certain standards in order to obtain their accreditation.

American College Testing Program (ACT): An aptitude test administered to secondary students in 11th or 12th grade students to help determine capability for postsecondary study. It assesses the student's ability in reading, mathematics, English language and science skills and an optional writing sample.

Adequate Yearly Progress (AYP): An individual state's measure of yearly progress toward achieving state academic standards. "Adequate Yearly Progress" is the minimum level of improvement that states, school districts and schools must achieve each year.

Benchmark tests: A term given to the test given after a specific course to assess the knowledge learned during the course. Oftentimes, passing of the test is required for entrance into the next grade level or course. Under No Child Left Behind, tests are aligned with academic standards. Beginning in the 2002-03 school year, schools must administer tests in each of three grade spans: grades 3-5, grades 6-9, and grades 10-12 in all schools. Beginning in the 2005-06 school year, tests must be administered every year in grades 3 through 8 in math and reading. Beginning in the 2007-08 school year, science achievement must also be tested.

Centers: An educational approach that consists of approximately 3-12 centers of varying subjects (i.e. science, computer, and handwriting). Centers usually last about an hour during which students can go to 2-3 centers each day. The purpose of the centers is to teach a variety of topics at once while enhancing the students' independence with their work.

Charter School: A tax-supported public school that is designed and operated by educators, parents, community leaders, educational entrepreneurs, and others. They are sponsored by designated local or state educational organizations, who monitor their quality and effectiveness but allow them to operate outside of the traditional system of public schools.

Comprehension: The ability to understand and gain meaning from what has been read.

Corrective Action: When a school or school district does not make yearly progress, the state will place it under a "Corrective Action Plan." The plan will include resources to improve teaching, administration, or curriculum. If a school continues to be identified as in need of improvement, then the state has increased authority to make any necessary, additional changes to ensure improvement.

Criterion-referenced testing: A test in which questions are chosen according to specific predetermined criteria. A student's scores are based upon his knowledge and mastery of a certain skill.

Curriculum Night: A night designed for teachers to share with the parents about the grade level standards, procedures, and events. Curriculum Night differs from personal conferences in that it is a whole group event. Any questions should pertain to the whole group rather than the individual.

Curriculum Standards: Each state is required to follow certain standards to help guide classroom instruction as well as receive federal assistance. The standards are broken up by grade level, then each subject has its own set of standards that educators use to guide the classroom instruction. For example, in fifth grade, one math standard states that the "students will understand congruence of geometric figures and the correspondence of their vertices, sides, and angles."

Differentiation: The modification of curriculum and instruction according to content, pacing, and/or product to meet the unique needs of the students in the classroom.

Distinguished Schools: Awards given to schools when they make major gains in achievement.

Early Intervention Program (EIP): A small-group instructional setting designed for young children who require improvement in specific content area. Strategies vary and depend on the specific needs of each child, and are most often decided upon by a team of the parents, teachers, and administrators.

Fluency: The capacity to read text accurately and quickly.

Gifted program: Usually given various titles depending on the school. The gifted programs are designed for the students who are excelling in the regular classroom curriculum. On top of the normal classroom work, the gifted program provides the excelling students with extension work, technology projects, and/or enrichment activities. Usually a request from both the parents and teacher is required for entrance into the program.

Individualized Education Program (IEP): A personalized list of strategies and tools to use for a struggling student, usually designed by the student's parents, teachers, and administration. The IEP is a direct result of the IDEA law that was re-established in 2004.

Individuals with Disabilities Education Act (IDEA):
A law, established in 1975 and re-established in 2004, to ensure services to children with disabilities throughout the nation. IDEA governs how states and public agencies provide early intervention and special education.

Magnet School: A tax-supported public school that offers a specific or enhanced curriculum designed for students of special interest or ability.

Mission/Philosophy: A statement outlining the guidelines a school follows to achieve its goals or maintain performance standards.

Montessori: A school designed around the principles of Dr. Maria Montessori, whose methodology focused on the unique individuality, self-reliance, and independence of nursery and elementary-aged children.

Norm-referenced testing: An assessment that compares an individual's results with a large group of individuals who have taken the same assessment (who are referred to as the "norming group"). Examples include the SAT and Iowa Tests of Basic Skills.

Open House: An event held at a school and open to the public, at which parents can learn more about the school and its offerings. Usually the Open House occurs between the months of October and March.

No Child Left Behind: A federal law passes in 2001 designed to ensure that all children have a fair and equal opportunity to obtain a high quality education and meet state academic standards of proficiency.

Notification Deadline: The date by which a private school notifies families of the acceptance of a child in the enrollment to the school.

Phonemic Awareness: The ability to hear and identify individual sounds (called phonemes) in spoken words.

Phonics: The relationship between letters and their sounds.

Preliminary SAT/National Merit Scholarship Qualifying Test (PSAT/NMSQT): A voluntary test given to secondary school students in 10th or 11th grade to assist them in preparing for the SAT and to qualify for national merit scholarships. It assesses the student's ability in reading, writing, and mathematical problem-solving skills.

Reply Deadline: The date by which parents must notify an accepting private school of their commitment to enroll their child.

Response to Intervention (RTI): A strategy developed after the reauthorization of IDEA. The goal of RTI is to work with children experiencing academic and/or behavioral difficulties and identify their specific needs. The specific strategies and enrichment activities are based upon the individual student's needs and expectations.

Scholastic Aptitude Test (SAT): An aptitude test administered to secondary students in 11th and 12th grade to help determine capability for postsecondary study. It is divided into two parts, the SAT Reasoning Test measuring reading, writing and quantitative skills; and the SAT Subject Tests measuring knowledge and reasoning ability in various subjects.

Secondary School Admissions Test (SSAT): An aptitude test frequently administered to students applying to private secondary schools and some public secondary schools. It measures verbal, reading, and quantitative skills and also includes a writing sample.

Special Needs School: A school or program focusing on the needs of children who have mild to moderate learning disabilities. The school usually has smaller class sizes, individualized attention, and multi-sensory learning methods.

Standardized tests: While the name of the test varies from state to state, the core remains the same. Standardized tests are scientifically normed and machine-graded instruments administered to students under controlled conditions to assess capabilities, including knowledge, cognitive skills and abilities, and aptitude. They are used extensively in the U.S. education system at all levels to assist with admissions, placement, and counseling decisions. Some of these tests include a written portion that is hand-graded.

Standards-based report cards: Report cards that display the mastery of a student's progress of a specific learning skill (or standard). After being tested on the skill, it is determined if the student:

1. Does not meet the standard
2. Partially meets the standard
3. Meets the standard or
4. Exceeds the standard.

Student Support Team (SST): A team of guidance counselors, general education teachers, administrators, other support staff, and, sometimes the parents, used to collaborate and discuss a student's needs and identify academic and behavioral interventions and supports that the teacher may implement to help the student achieve. The SST is designed to provide assistance to teachers as they work with students who are experiencing difficulties academically and/or behaviorally. The SST process is data-driven. SST members consider evidence that the teacher collects to document the concern; they also design an implementation plan that includes a monitoring and evaluation component to determine the effectiveness of the intervention.

Teacher of the Year: A prestigious award given to one teacher from each school as elected by the fellow teachers and staff based on the individual teacher's outstanding teaching ability. After receiving the school Teacher of the Year award, a county-level and statewide Teacher of the Year is then chosen by a select panel of judges from the state. From the state Teachers of the Year, the National Teacher of the Year is selected and is presented to the national public by the president of the United States. The National Teacher of the Year is released from classroom duties during the year of recognition to travel nationally and internationally as a spokesperson for the teaching profession.

Test of English as a Foreign Language (TOEFL): A proficiency test designed to measure knowledge and skill in understanding and using the English language. It is required of international students whose native language or previous language of instruction was not English, and some U.S. institutions will accept TOEFL scores in lieu of other test scores.

Title 1: Refers to programs aimed at America's most disadvantaged students. It provides assistance to improve the teaching and learning of children in high-poverty schools to enable those children to meet challenging State academic content and performance standards. Title I reaches about 12.5 million students enrolled in both public and private schools.

Vocabulary: The words students must know to read effectively.

Unfortunately these terms are constantly changing. The educational world is always looking for the next "hot topic" solution to improve education. The best way to keep up with the terms is to look on your state's Board of Education website, the National Board of Education website, or, when all else fails, just ask a teacher!

"Glossary of Terms." US Department of Education. July 22, 2004. Web.

About The Authors

Tiffany Andrews

Graduated from the University of Georgia with a degree in Early
Childhood Education for grades K-5. Afterwards she taught kindergarten
for three years and served as the Department Head for kindergarten and
Pre-K. Currently Tiffany teaches 2nd grade, and she resides near Lake
Lanier, GA with her husband Chase.

Becky Saarela

Attended both Bethel College and John Brown University and graduated
with a degree in Home Economics for grades K-12. Becky taught Home
Economics in Illinois for seven years but after moving to Georgia she
took a break from teaching to raise her two daughters, Heather and
Tiffany. When her daughters were both in school Becky worked as a
substitute teacher and later as a paraprofessional in a middle school
special education classroom. Currently Becky teaches Nutrition and
Wellness and Food Science. Becky has also served several years as her
high school's cheerleading and girls lacrosse coach.